Ordering Information

The paperback sourcebooks listed below are published quarterly and can be ordered either by subscription or single-copy.

Subscriptions cost $35.00 per year for institutions, agencies, and libraries. Individuals can subscribe at the special rate of $21.00 per year *if payment is by personal check.* (Note that the full rate of $35.00 applies if payment is by institutional check, even if the subscription is designated for an individual.) Standing orders are accepted. Subscriptions normally begin with the first of the four sourcebooks in the current publication year of the series. When ordering, please indicate if you prefer your subscription to begin with the first issue of the *coming* year.

Single copies are available at $7.95 when payment accompanies order, and *all single-copy orders under $25.00 must include payment.* (California, New Jersey, New York, and Washington, D.C., residents please include appropriate sales tax.) For billed orders, cost per copy is $7.95 plus postage and handling. (Prices subject to change without notice.)

Bulk orders (ten or more copies) of any individual sourcebook are available at the following discounted prices: 10–49 copies, $7.15 each; 50–100 copies, $6.35 each; over 100 copies, *inquire.* Sales tax and postage and handling charges apply as for single copy orders.

To ensure correct and prompt delivery, all orders must give either the *name of an individual* or an *official purchase order number.* Please submit your order as follows:

Subscriptions: specify series and year subscription is to begin.
Single Copies: specify sourcebook code (such as, TL8) and first two words of title.

Mail orders for United States and Possessions, Latin America, Canada, Japan, Australia, and New Zealand to:
Jossey-Bass Inc., Publishers
433 California Street
San Francisco, California 94104

Mail orders for all other parts of the world to:
Jossey-Bass Limited
28 Banner Street
London EC1Y 8QE

New Directions for Teaching and Learning Series
Kenneth E. Eble and John F. Noonan, *Editors-in-Chief*

Contents

Editors' Notes

At the end of the third decade since educators have been charged with the mission of providing equal opportunity in education, it is time to check our course, update our methods, and question the deliberateness of our speed. What happened to the promises held out by the lofty rhetoric of the 1950s and 1960s? The authors of the chapters in this volume discuss their efforts as educators to honor those promises. Here you will find fresh approaches to old hopes: How can colleges educate all students to their potential? How can colleges undo the impact of racism on faculty and students? How can we prepare students to live and work effectively in a multiracial society? While the volume focuses on racial minority students, especially blacks, the authors believe that every student can benefit from the practices advocated here.

In Chapter One, Ronald W. Saufley, Kathryn O. Cowan, and J. Herman Blake describe the challenges that minority students face in predominantly white institutions. In Chapter Two, Jacquelyn Mitchell discusses minority faculty who must balance conflicting allegiances in their efforts to integrate dual perspectives. In Chapter Three, Joseph Katz writes about white faculty who are trying to focus on the effects of racism on their teaching.

The next three chapters give readers specific ideas for improving teaching effectiveness with minority students. In Chapter Four, William E. Sedlacek draws on his extensive research into the noncognitive variables that lead to success for minority students and suggests how faculty can use those variables in their teaching. In Chapter Five, Jean Wu and Kiyo Morimoto present their views on listening to minority students. In Chapter Six, Lillian C. McDermott, Mark L. Rosenquist, and Emily H. van Zee explore the difficulties that minority students often face in the sciences and describe teaching strategies for addressing those difficulties.

Administrators and faculty development consultants may be particularly interested in the suggestions presented by the authors of the last three chapters. In Chapter Seven, James Cones, Denise Janha, and Jack Noonan describe their work with white faculty who are examining their assumptions about teaching black students. In Chapter Eight, Alvin D. Rivera describes an academic support structure designed to help Hispanic students help other Hispanic students to prepare for

2

technical careers. Finally, in Chapter Nine, James Cones offers a perspective that may encourage faculty and administrators not to abandon their struggle to teach minority students.

James H. Cones, III
John F. Noonan
Denise Janha
Editors

James H. Cones, III, is a graduate assistant at the Center for Improving Teaching Effectiveness (CITE), Virginia Commonwealth University.

Denise Janha is assistant director of CITE.

John F. Noonan, former director of CITE, is dean of arts and science at Iona College, New Rochelle, New York.

Convinced that they do not belong at the predominantly white university, many minority students enter to find their worst fears and self-doubts immediately and forcefully confirmed.

The Struggles of Minority Students at Predominantly White Institutions

Ronald W. Saufley
Kathryn O. Cowan
J. Herman Blake

As higher education continues to increase the number of minority students enrolled in colleges and universities, it faces new challenges. These challenges come not only as the result of greater minority participation but from the assumptions that such students bring to the university. In the past, the few who came had often lived in or at least moved through the majority culture. Whether these students were at home in the university or not, they did at least recognize the system, and they had some idea of how to work within it. Now, many first-generation minority college students come to academia straight from the world of the barrio or the ghetto. Entering the university means not

The research on which this chapter is based was funded by a program grant from the Carnegie Corporation, and we wish to express our gratitude for its generous support. There is no implication of Carnegie Corporation endorsement of the views expressed in this chapter.

J. H. Cones, III, J. F. Noonan, D. Janha (Eds.). *Teaching Minority Students.* New Directions for Teaching and Learning, no. 16. San Francisco: Jossey-Bass, December 1983.

3

only that they must leave home for an unfamiliar academic setting but that they also must enter an alien social and physical environment that they, their family, and their peers have never experienced. They are faced with leaving a certain world in which they fit for an uncertain world where they already know that they do not fit.

This chapter grows out of an extended research project (Cowan and others, 1980) that analyzed the experience of new students at the university. The term *new student* was used to designate students from groups that traditionally have been denied access to higher education or from families in which they are the first member to attend college. Racial and ethnic minorities, some women, older students, and low-income students comprise this group of students. The designation *new student* was preferred to such terms as *disadvantaged* or *nontraditional* because the conventional terms promote the self-fulfilling negativism that tends to invalidate students. *New student* is a positive concept that acknowledges the strengths and unique qualities of these students without minimizing their academic deficiencies. Much of what follows is predicated on an understanding of the social-psychological state of such students on entrance to the university.

Coming to the University

Our prior research showed that, before coming to the university, many minority students were not only acutely aware of their academic deficiencies but had little hope of overcoming them. They had been systematically invalidated as persons with academic potential, they had very negative academic self-images, and they were highly fearful of the academic setting. Often, they were beset by guilt for leaving the family and for utilizing precious family resources. Their expectations of the university experience were shaped in part by a view of bureaucracy as a means of social control. They expected to confront an enemy in the system itself. Often, this perception seemed to be confirmed. Perhaps most important, many students had deeply internalized the feeling that they did not belong at the university and that they were almost certainly destined to fail there.

On the Campus

When the minority student besieged by such negative influences arrives at the university, the doubts are immediately reinforced. Isolation, alienation, nonacceptance, inadequate preparation, apparent racism, bureaucratic tangles, and unfamiliarity with the system combine to restrict the student further and often produce devastating patterns of behavior guaranteed to fulfill a personal prophecy of failure.

At many campuses, the first thing that minority students notice is that there are very few other minority students on campus. Students who have never before lived in the majority culture find that critical mass of their own kind is lacking. The small numbers and the resulting isolation tend to underline the negative aspects of minority status and reconfirm that the university was not built for them and that they do not belong. When such isolation is doubled by separation from a supportive cultural community, as it is at our rural campus, the isolation can also begin the process of alienating the students from themselves. As the students are removed from the comfort of the home community, which allows them to define themselves in positive terms in relation to their immediate world, they are ultimately removed from comfort with self, a circumstance that heightens their self-doubts and fears.

The uniqueness and apartness of these students are further emphasized by the general patterns of living around them. Life-style differences are exacerbated when diverse cultures and backgrounds are brought together under one roof. Economic class differences are accentuated. Surrounded by affluence, the minority student is often angered by "extravagance" that reconfirms the perception of not belonging. Activities geared to the traditional population—the campus newspaper, cultural activities, lectures, dances—have a ripple effect on students as their social separateness is intensively felt.

Feeling cut off from the larger life of the university around them, minority students often feel forced to create their own tight social world. This can cause them to miss out on the larger potential of the university. In such internal communities, gossip or the grapevine are not only a means of communication, but they can become a form of social control. At colleges where minority females greatly outnumber minority males, women who may be forced to be friends socially find themselves competing fiercely for males, which undermines the very foundation of the supportive community. The resulting tension further heightens students' discomfort and reemphasizes the perception that they do not belong.

Racism. Against the background of previous experiences with the larger society and the overwhelming evidence that they do not belong at the university, minority students must confront the specter of racism. Admittedly, some students may be ultrasensitive to the issue— they have had to develop such sensitivity as a survival strategy—but there are enough manifestations of the phenomenon that the students' preconceptions seem to be validated.

Particularly among other students but to a surprising degree among administrators and some faculty as well, minority students encounter an assumption that the system now coddles their kind. It is assumed and often overtly expressed by others that minorities get positions whether they are qualified or not, that preferential treatment is accorded them throughout the system, and that all minority students receive financial aid. In light of the desperate financial situation of many minority students, the last attitude is particularly upsetting.

What is interpreted as overt racism is also evidenced by the difficulty that many majority students experience in their attempts to mingle or associate with minority students. (The reverse also holds true to far too great a degree.) When majority students are willing to mingle, many manifest inappropriate racial attitudes, which are disclosed in their assumptions or questions about other cultures and lifestyles. Even if their remarks are not overtly racist, majority students can display appalling ignorance and insensitivity in their comments on such areas as food, violence, sex, and poverty and in their belief that all minorities are poor and come only from the ghetto.

On our campus, one of the most frequent examples of hostility cited by minority students is what we have come to call the *hate stare*. This phenomenon has been described by so many different students that it cannot be interpreted as an effect of oversensitivity. Difficult to describe, the hate stare is most often found in particular parts of campus where the majority culture is well entrenched and segregated. The hate stare is used actively and aggressively to discomfit minority students in an attempt to drive them out of traditional bastions. Here is how one male student described it: "I go to study in [another college's] library, and, I swear to God, I've never seen so many people staring at me. It got to the point where I didn't want to go to their library by myself. So I told R., 'Come with me, and we'll check it out.' So, we went. We were studying... This Anglo person comes up eating an apple, savage-like, saliva running down his mouth. He looked in the window, and he looked at me, and I looked down and kept on writing. Then he came in and stood right in front of the table and just stared at us. He finished the apple and left the apple core on the table and just kept staring. R. goes, 'Can we help you?' He just looked with a dirty look and just walked away." While such behavior is generally not reported in classroom settings, it occurs often enough in academically related areas that minority students assume that it also represents how they will be viewed in the classroom.

While overt racism is reported less often in the classroom than in other campus settings, it occurs often enough to keep minority students on the edge and cause them to "find" racism in cases where perhaps it does not exist. Such comments as that of the teaching assistant who asks, "Is English your primary language?" or the teacher who states, "You guys"—by which the teacher means *you minorities*—"have it so easy, now I'm going to show you what it's like to work" reconfirm the students' conception of the system itself as racist. Under such conditions, innocent statements by a sympathetic faculty member can be seen as further proof that even the best are racist. (This happened some years ago to one of the most committed and empathetic faculty members on campus, who used the word *niggardly* in a lecture on nineteenth-century U.S. fiscal policy.)

Thus, minority students see themselves thrust into a hostile and often racist system in which they must not only go to school but live. They experience an unrelenting tension that places them on guard twenty-four hours a day. One cannot even go down the hall to the bathroom comfortably, "'cause you may have to deal with it."

Family Pressures. Generally, minority students are extremely concerned about the well-being of their family, which can create a conflict of interest between the student's scholastic needs and the family's needs. The very strengths that have enabled the student to reach college can cause the family to rely on the student for moral support, conflict mediation, financial assistance, and advice. The student is caught in a double bind: If the student acts in the family's interest, studies suffer; if the student does not, the student can be consumed by guilt, particularly if the family is sacrificing to help the student through school or if the family has opposed the student's matriculation. Also, while the student's feeling that he or she has to succeed for the family or to serve as a role model for others in the family can be motivating, it also helps to sustain pressure than can ultimately be enervating.

Family pressures can be further exacerbated by financial considerations. Guilt is a common response among students who know that their family must sacrifice basic necessities or rare luxury items in order to enable them to attend college. They are very fearful of wasting valuable family resources. For others, pleas by parents to stay home and work to contribute to family income impose a large measure of guilt. As a result, many students send portions of their financial aid monies home. These students can be so preoccupied by financial concerns that their classroom performance is hampered.

The minority student who enters the classroom with so many internal pressures is then confronted by the traditional student, who seems to be articulate and aggressive, to write reasonably well, and be comfortable with the bureaucracy. The apparent contrast heightens the negative self-image and conforms the minority student's doubts about his or her ability to succeed at the university. The most common response is overwhelming fear. While this fear is sometimes manifest in outward forms of behavior, such as brashness or antagonism, the internal consequences are ultimately almost paralyzing.

In the Classroom

On entering the classroom, many minority students are acutely aware of their alienation, isolation, and inadequate preparation. They feel enormous pressure, they feel intimidated, and they are often afraid to ask questions or engage in dialogue. Immediate academic paralysis is a common response. One of the most eloquent examples of this experience was articulated to us by a successful senior who still experienced these powerful emotions after four years: "I remember how nervous I was. My face got hot. My hands shook. I would put my hands under the table so no one could see. I felt so threatened, and I used to go see [the counselors]. I have always felt suffocated by being inhibited—felt oppressed by my lack of articulateness. Growth for me was very important. [But,] I was so frustrated at not being able to grasp the material. It was like a foreign language. The readings were like holding my breath and diving into ten feet of water."

At the same time, the student also manifests a fear of being judged stupid or academically unfit, which further confirms the expectation of failure. This fear often leads such students not to be assertive in class—sometimes even to refuse to participate at all in class dialogue, even when the student suspects that he or she has something important to say. The professor may then interpret the student's failure to participate as proof of the student's lack of class preparation or lack of interest in the course material.

The predicament is further compounded for students for whom English is a second language or for students who are aware of the predominance of street vernacular in their language, which they know will be judged as inappropriate to the academic setting. Some students who are willing to risk classroom dialogue report that they are so concerned with being articulate (in this case, they mean with achieving mechanical perfection) that they lose the essence of their arguments: Thus, in the interest of conforming to one set of university standards, they seem to violate another. The fear of verbal interaction can become so pronounced that it influences a student's entire course of study: For example, one minority woman at our school majored and graduated in mathematics—which she hated—solely in order to escape verbal discourse. The problem is further aggravated for many minority students by the lack of adequate writing skills. Acutely aware of their weaknesses, they have grave self-doubts about whether they can ever learn to express themselves on paper. This fear is particularly acute for some bilingual students, who feel uncomfortable writing in either language.

Given all this inner turmoil and the inordinate pressures under which minority students are forced to work, it is clear that students need help. However, several factors can mitigate against their seeking such assistance. Some students fear that they will only conform the view that they do not belong at the university in the first place or that they will show how far behind they have fallen. Some are afraid of asking for help from better prepared students for fear of holding the others back. Others become prey to the systemic individualism fostered by the university—you must do it on your own; knowledge is self-acquired—without seeing that a whole cooperative network has helped the traditional students to get where they are. Some minority students—particularly where sophisticated written work is involved—are highly skeptical of being placed in situations where white tutors act as judges of their initial attempts to prepare written assignments.

The problems are further exacerbated by the study habits of many minority students. In some cases, particularly for students whose goals are unclear, the issue of study self-discipline is paramount. For most, however, the issue becomes not so much one of how much time is put into a class but rather of how that time is used. They can put in an extraordinary number of hours, but because their study skills are deficient they find that they have acquired very little for their efforts. They know what they want, but they do not necessarily know how to get it. This only serves to feed their self-doubts.

With all this going on internally, a seemingly minor event—one that appears to be completely innocuous to the outside observer—may suddenly focus all the negatives for the student and dictate a pattern of behavior that assures the student's prophecy of failure. For example, a young male student who had been performing quite well at our university was asked to prepare and give a small oral report. He dreaded the assignment—because of his English pronunciation. Since he had been laughed at in other situations, he decided not to go to the class for which his presentation was scheduled. He then became fearful of returning to class at all, and got so far behind that he became suicidal. Ultimately, the student's discomfort became so unbearable that he dropped out.

Responses to the Class Situation

Students evidence a variety of responses to their systematic academic invalidation and to the pressures and fears that they feel at the university. We are all familiar with the brashness, bravado, or aggressiveness that some students display in an attempt to cover deep-seated feelings of insecurity. Many attack the system verbally and blame others for their difficulties. If these students are pressed, however, we find that many are angry with themselves. Such self-directed anger can further alienate these students from self and accentuate the cycle of negatives.

While many behavioral patterns of minority students are readily observable and quite well understood, two particularly complex phenomena need further elucidation. We have termed them the *ultimate doom syndrome* and the *getting-over syndrome*.

The Ultimate Doom Syndrome. Students who experience the ultimate doom syndrome are characterized by fear of the future. They become convinced that failure is certain. Even if such students overcome the initial buffeting in the university and begin to negotiate the system, they are so certain that failure must eventually result that their only question is when it will occur and in what form. The student may be perfectly aware that he or she is doing well for the time being, but moving through the university serves only to bring the student closer to ultimate catastrophe. This student views each academic success not as proof that he or she can make it but that the ultimate failure is near. Hence, what others view as indicators that the student can succeed has the opposite effect: It heightens the student's anxiety and increases the pressure.

Students who suffer from the ultimate doom syndrome are characterized by ambivalence toward their success in college. In spite of passing courses or getting good evaluations, they still harbor grave doubts about their ability to succeed. They often seem unable to project successful performances to further successes, and they may seriously underestimate their achievements and their progress.

The Getting-Over Syndrome. *Getting over* is a ghetto term for beating the system or for achieving success by doing as little as possible that the system requires. The getting-over syndrome is fairly common among minority students. For some, it is precisely what it appears to be: a conscious, active manipulation of the system for tangible rewards at the expense of little effort. For others, however, the seeming cynicism is actually a fearful self-protective device employed in response to absolute certainty of failure.

While getting-over behavior may have begun in the barrio or the ghetto as a means of manipulating a hostile system, what started the syndrome is not necessarily what sustains it. For many minority students, the syndrome serves as protection against the conclusion that would have otherwise to be drawn from the failure that these students are certain will occur. These students engage in patterns of behavior that do not challenge their doubts and fears if by some miracle they are successful—Can I do it? I didn't have to find out. If they are unsuccessful, the doubts and fears remain unchallenged—Since I didn't really try, my failure doesn't prove that I couldn't do it; I didn't really fail, I just didn't play their game. Psychologically, the student has set up a no lose situation. A poignant example of the process at work can be found in the words of a second-year student at our institution: "I have a fear of failing, and what I tend to do is not to take on the challenge—to defeat myself before I have even tried to see whether I can do it. My fears are holding me back."

Getting-over students generally are bright, capable, and aware, and the public postures that they assume stand in stark contrast to their internal insecurities and fears. They appear to be self-assured, confident, even nonchalant, while they may exhibit a disinterested or even a hostile attitude. They seem—and in one respect they actually are—highly ambitious, but they are almost universally characterized by unclear goals. They frequently change their minds about long-range goals, switch majors, or drop courses.

Their obvious abilities and their self-assured image, coupled with their failure to produce satisfactory results, often lead them to be labeled as disinterested or lazy when in fact they are paralyzed by fear. When pressed by sensitive observers, getting-over students are able to recognize and articulate their lack of motivation. Generally, they are obsessed by the problem, which they do not know how to resolve. Outwardly, getting-over students tend to externalize the problem—the classes are irrelevant, the teacher is boring, the readings are dull, the material does not relate to life, there are too many outside distractions—expecting motivation to come from sources outside themselves. They often contend that abstract ideas are unimportant or that they have no relevance to their lives.

Getting-over students frequently do not know how to resolve their problem. They assume that they will naturally emerge from their lack of motivation and that the resultant lethargy will pass. All express optimism at the beginning of each new school term, discussing high hopes and expectations regarding buckling down, self-discipline, and study habits. However, they are seldom able to offer concrete plans for accomplishing these changes, and as the term progresses and they fail in their intentions, they begin to project on to the next term and frantically try to manipulate the system to cover themselves for the immediate term.

The result of getting-over behavior, then, is a skewed continuation of low-performance patterns developed by bright, capable students in the precollege years in response to a system that has low expectations for such students. This pattern is extremely hard to overcome.

Alienation. For many students from the barrio or the ghetto who are able to persevere through all the difficulties posed by the university, another anxiety lies in wait. These students begin to become aware of their ultimate alienation from their home community and their own culture. This alienation from the community alienates them further from themselves as the students' cultural support systems are eroded. Some drop out and return to the community. Others, recognizing the limited range of opportunities available if they do return, choose to go on, but in so choosing they are aware of the implied negative self-criticisms of their past. The reasoning goes something like this: If I am to reach new horizons, I must break the patterns of my past. While I can choose what I want to be, the one thing that I cannot be is what I was raised to be. As one male student phrased it, "I know what I'm coming from, but I don't know what I'm going to."

Students experiencing alienation become increasingly aware that they can no longer simply return unchanged to the home community. They find that their ideas have changed and that everyone comments on how they have changed, and they find they are often critical of the home community in ways that they have not experienced previously. They find that they have lost contact with their friends, that common interests have gone, that their values have changed, that they are out of touch with styles and the grapevine. In essence, they find that they are no longer an integral part of the social fabric that nurtured them, although being a part of that fabric remains their strongest desire.

Uncomfortable and alienated at the university and ultimately acknowledging that they will become severely alienated from their home community, these students suddenly find that they do not belong anywhere. The more successful that these students become at the university, the greater the alienation and the greater the resulting discomfort and anxiety. Alienated students become marginal persons. Having defined the world in bipolar opposites, such students live in two worlds, recognizing that they really fit into neither. Moving back and forth between the two worlds, these students generally find it impossible to relate one world to the other, and they may be pulled apart and disoriented as a result. These students are caught in a push-pull situation: pushed by the university toward expanding opportunities that are unclear and uncertain, pulled by the home that is clear and certain but limited. The fear and guilt that arise from leaving the known and comfortable can produce excruciating social and psychological problems that lead to poor performance or dropout.

Moreover, while the student's previous social fabric of support and comfort is being discarded, it is not being replaced at the university with adequate support systems. Also, the student's goals and options often remain hazy and undefined, so that while the student may find it liberating to realize that his or her range of choices has greatly expanded, the student's anxiety level is increased by not knowing exactly what he or she is choosing.

Student Strengths

Although minority students are burdened with inordinate and exceptional pressures as they move through the traditional university, they can make it, and they are doing so in ever increasing numbers when they are given sufficient opportunity. In the struggle, they exhibit several basic strengths vital to their success. These strengths are often overlooked by those who work in higher education. At our institution, we have had a rather unique opportunity to observe various student growth patterns, as the rural, isolated nature of our residential campus puts us in unusually close contact with most students for a considerable period of time. Several of us live and work with students on a twenty-four-hours-a-day basis, leading many students to share their perspectives with us in ways that otherwise might not be possible. As a result, we have begun to see the dim outlines of the positive qualities that many minority students bring to academia, which enable them ultimately to prevail against seemingly overwhelming odds.

Perhaps most important, minority students are generally characterized by strong commitment—not always to higher education at first but to positive social changes in their home community, which they see themselves as helping to effect. With the assistance of sensitive college teachers, that powerful commitment to change can give rise to an equally strong commitment to the educational process, as the student comes to see the university as a primary way of arming oneself for a lifelong social struggle.

Minority students are also generally characterized by an amazing perseverence born over many years of struggle with a basically hostile social system. By the odds, they should not be where they are — but they are. If they are given a chance to see that they can succeed at the university, they exhibit a tenacious determination to work through or to beat the system. While they sometimes experience academic defeat, they are extremely resilient, returning again and again to the struggle when they have the opportunity. For example, our college — one of eight on campus — has an approximately 50 percent lower-economic-class minority enrollment. It has the lowest graduation rate after four years but the highest graduation rate after six years.

Minority students are also adaptable. They have had to be, in order to get through the system. Although the traditional university may be initially foreign to them and while it may never become quite comfortable, minority students can make the exceedingly difficult transition and find it a positive experience when they are given time to discover that the university can be an ally, not just another invalidating agency of social control.

We have also found that the marginality so devastating to younger students can become a strength for older students, for whom it serves as a source of new creativity and insight. Indeed, as students broaden their perspective and develop more comprehensive literary tools and analytical skills, the "marginal person" phenomenon can actually become an asset, as the dual alienation of students from their own past and from the university produces a creative tension that enables them to examine old questions in new and exciting ways. We have found this to be particularly true for several former students whom we have been able to follow through their graduate school career.

Conclusion

In the final analysis, we must recognize that isolated and alienated minority students occupy an exceptionally precarious position at most predominantly white universities. If we at the university are sincere about wanting to increase the numbers and participation of such students in our schools, we must be willing to approach the challenge with considerably more sensitivity, insight, and willingness to change than we have exhibited in the past.

Reference

Cowan, K. O., Saufley, F. W., and Blake, J. H. "Through the Hourglass (Darkly)." Unpublished paper, 1980. Portions of this paper were presented in seminars at the Educational Testing Service, Princeton, N.J., April 1980; Brown University, Providence, R.I., May 1980; and the California Postsecondary Education Commission, Sacramento, July 1982.

Ronald W. Saufley is planning officer and coordinator of student support services at Oakes College, University of California, Santa Cruz (UCSC). Oakes is a highly diverse, multiracial college founded specifically to incorporate more new students — particularly minority students — into the university system.

Kathryn O. Cowan did much of the interviewing on which the study reported in this chapter was based; she is currently with the University Relations Department at UCSC.

J. Herman Blake is provost of Oakes College and professor of sociology at UCSC.

Although minority professors in predominately white universities are immersed in systems of dual expectations, rules, and judgments created by institution and ethnic community, they can be viable members of both systems.

Visible, Vulnerable, and Viable: Emerging Perspectives of a Minority Professor

Jacquelyn Mitchell

The presence today of many minority faculty members on college and university campuses represents the most recent stage of a historic movement to eliminate the legal barriers to full citizenship erected by race, creed, or prior state of servitude. This movement was animated by a sense of the injustice perpetuated by legislation and social sentiment that systematically excluded members of certain racial and ethnic groups from access to educational facilities that could enable them to realize their potential and to enjoy their rights as American citizens. Largely through the efforts of the National Association for the Advancement of Colored People (NAACP), de jure segregation of graduate and professional education was formally ended in the early 1950s. Following this success, the NAACP, armed with sociological and psychological research findings, successfully challenged the doctrine of separate but equal educational facilities in elementary schools. The Supreme Court ruled in the classic 1954 *Brown* vs. *Board of Education of Topeka* case that separate but equal was inherently unequal and therefore unconstitutional. Schools were mandated to integrate with all

J. H. Cones, III, J. F. Noonan, D. Janha (Eds.). *Teaching Minority Students.* New Directions for Teaching and Learning, no. 16. San Francisco: Jossey-Bass, December 1983.

deliberate speed. As a result of this decree, many minority children found themselves thrust into experimental integrated educational settings that espoused culturally incongruent philosophical and social ideologies.

The tactics devised to accomplish the legal mandate placed many students in integrated settings. Formal inclusion in the majority school culture was intended to counteract the exclusionary legacy of past practices. However, student differences — racial, ethnic, linguistic, and economic — became salient markers that kept the newcomers apart from the culture that they had integrated. While busing became symbolic of the intrusion of government into the private realm of neighborhoods and schools, the children who rode the buses and attended the schools experienced a new form of visibility that made them vulnerable in ways that previous generations had not experienced. Media treatment of the civil rights movement caused even children who did not participate directly in busing programs to experience this new visibility.

Thrust into a variety of programs promising new opportunities, minority students became the pawns in the battle of an egalitarian society with its heritage of discriminating practices and prejudicial attitudes. Schools became the major battlefront as the rhetoric of equality advocated educational correctives for the traditions of inequality embedded in social structure. Compensatory education became the means, but its consequences served only to highlight for students the social ambiguities implicit in the notion of compensation.

Frequently, economic boundaries were crossed in order to integrate schools, and minority students paid a penalty for not having the same economic benefits as their white peers. Many discovered that the cultural norms of their respective communities were evaluated negatively in schools, and their dialects and behaviors were often the source of derision. At the same time, they learned that their mere presence was potent enough to create a new phenomenon of rejection — white flight. But, the most subtle form of socialization in this new environment emerged with the school's use of so-called objective tests that created new forms of internal segregation.

Minority students viewed what the schools saw as grouping by ability somewhat differently, since those in the special education and language remediation programs were primarily black, Native American, and Hispanic peers. The explanations proffered by experts for the poor performance of minority students on standardized tests intensified the discrepancy between the rhetoric and the reality of integration. Families that invested heavily in their children's future only to see them geographically and culturally transferred to a different world found themselves called the cause of their children's failure.

To students whose academic ability was confirmed by the objective criteria of schools, the rhetoric of equality through education held out special promise and a different form of contradiction. Their ability to conform to the norms associated with the dominant culture suggested that they departed from the norms associated with their ethnicity. Although education enlightens, it cannot whiten technicolor reality. As these students came to see their success as rooted in their unique individuality, they frequently became estranged from their family and community. Yet, the knowledge that they gained made them aware that a large number of their peers who did not make it had been victims of societal conditions, not of lack of individual ability. They became frustrated by the inequities that turned many of their friends into combat soldiers in Vietnam, inmates in prisons, or workers in low-status occupations. For many, these contradictory experiences fostered a new consciousness in which individualism became the exception and collective experiences became the norm of their understanding of workings of society.

It is not surprising that many of those who entered college rebelled against the institutional labeling that denied their ethnic identity. Some substituted ethnic for egalitarian concerns and sought to devise new means of expressing their collective identity. Others fought for their right to participate in a variety of traditional areas of study that had excluded minorities. Individuals from both groups succeeded in qualifying as the new generation of Ph.D.s available for academic positions. Precisely because students in the second group succeeded in traditional fields, far less is known about their struggles, dilemmas, and despair than those who followed different routes. As former students holding the newly elevated status of professor, these exceptions — some might call them the fortunate ones — became at once minorities within the majority culture and minorities within their minority culture. Socialized to individualistic identities, these minority scholars also became accustomed, especially in the elite colleges and universities, to serving as conspicuous symbols in a setting that also contained all the problems associated with the professional role.

In moving from the role of student to that of professor, these scholars continued to function as pioneers but in a drastically different environment. Their environments were structured to some extent by their discipline and by the professors with whom they worked. However, the professional role required them to assume new authority and unfamiliar responsibilities.

While the experiences involved in mastering this new role can be described in terms of marginality, discontinuity, or dissonance, this chapter will examine the living experiences of scholars in the process of actively constructing their social reality as members both of their academic and of their ethnic community. To communicate this experience, I will characterize the process in terms of the tensions and challenges that one must confront in one's self and of the contradictions and limitations in communities and institutions that one must recognize and articulate.

This chapter will describe and examine my personal perspectives as a minority professor in three related domains: being visible, being vulnerable, and being viable in the white academic community — distinct phases that capture the complexity and contradictory nature of the roles in which we have been cast. Of course, the opinions and interpretations expressed in this chapter are mine and do not necessarily reflect those of other minority professors.

Visibility: Reflections

"I am invisible," says Ellison's (1972, p.3) Invisible Man, "because people refuse to see me. . . . as though I have been surrounded by mirrors of hard distorted glass. . . . You ache with the need to convince yourself that you do exist in the real world. . . . You curse and swear to make them recognize you. And, alas, it's seldom successful." For the aspiring nontraditional scholar, Ellison's masterful treatment of the paradoxical plight of the invisibility of the most visible is particularly poignant. While coming to see one's self as others do, the minority scholar often discovers that the hallowed halls of ivy are lined with strange reflections. From the initial interview for the position to the four-to-eight-year struggle for tenure, minority scholars confront dual systems of expectations, rules, and judgments from within their institution and from within their ethnic community.

Our physical appearance invariably evokes unconscious attitudes and unfounded presumptions regarding our competence as scholars and our viability as faculty members. It begins in university search committee meetings when faculty members view minority candidacy with fixed, biased convictions and are unable to separate issues of ethnicity from issues of qualification. The judgments continue throughout the recruiting process. Thus, minority applicants are penalized during recruitment procedures, and those who are hired remain minority members for the duration of their tenure in the minds of most other faculty.

To the minority applicant, competition for an academic position on the fair and open job market seems neither fair nor open, and university affirmative action hiring policies often seem perfunctory at best. Furthermore, "the most limited opportunities for status mobility among [minorities] call for stiffer competition than occurs among whites" (Ogbu, 1982, p. 427). In fact, minority scholars realize that their chances for securing a university appointment are significantly reduced unless ethnicity is clearly a prerequisite for the position. For example, a psychology department may be searching for a black psychologist, not for a psychologist who is black—a denotation considerably more meaningful than the semantic differences imply.

Even minority scholars selected for the final applicant pool regard their inclusion with caution, knowing that an invitation to come for an interview or to present a colloquium frequently means something other than it seems. While such an invitation may truly indicate genuine interest in and serious consideration of the applicant's candidacy, the minority applicant also recognizes that his or her presence on a campus as a viable candidate can be exploited to demonstrate the university's stated commitment to affirmative action goals. Invitations in such cases are a sham—nothing more than diversionary tactics to obscure actual intent. Ironically, the minority candidate who gets hired may also experience doubt, being unable to discern whether qualification or ethnicity was the decisive factor in his or her selection or whether it was both.

Inside the university, pressures associated with visibility reflect conflicting demands. Senior faculty and members of the administration warn minority scholars to place more emphasis on research and less on committee work and service obligations. Yet, many of the same people then ask, even urge, the minority scholar to get involved in recruiting a new faculty member, presenting a minority perspective in class or on a committee, counseling a minority student who has academic difficulties, or speaking to an outside group. The same people who evaluate the faculty member for advancement and for tenure ask these things seemingly unaware of the number of invitations that we must consider. Although "many of us resent this yoke . . . , [at] the same time [we] recognize our social responsibility to pursue and explain ethnic issues. Strangely enough, we often demand from ourselves what whites expect from us, while realizing the futility of accomplishing this goal to anyone's satisfaction" (Mitchell, 1982, p. 36).

Implicit in our visibility are the representative roles that we are forced to take. We are assumed to be less competent, yet we are also expected to replicate our white colleagues' output in both quantity and quality. We are chastised for spending excessive time with our students, but we are also relied on to reduce their isolation and cultural shock. We are criticized for participating in ethnically related community and university events, and we are given little recognition for our service contributions, but at the same time we are viewed as a critical link with the ethnic community.

Pressures regarding visibility and representation come also from the minority community. Poor communities have many needs and few people with clout. While such communities are often suspicious that minority faculty have lost interest in their affairs, they also request highly tangible services, such as membership on boards, assistance preparing applications for funding and grants, and advocacy for their children. Their needs are so immediate and their regard for the research process is so low that they often view refusal as an indication of snobbery or as a rejection of ethnic identity.

Typically, with few other minority faculty nearby as friends, relationships with minority students and with community people can both take on great importance and create conflicting demands. Our visibility affects both our professional and our personal life. Colleagues, community residents, and students react to it and develop perceptions about us because of it. Such perceptions, combined with the conflicts, demands of the role, and personal needs, create pressures that can jeopardize our health, happiness, and productivity. We become vulnerable to inner and outer demands by trying to create and maintain a feasible balance and meaningful synthesis of self, ethnicity, and profession—no small task.

Vulnerability: The Pitfalls of Reflections

DuBois (1961 [1903], pp. 16–17) evokes "a peculiar sensation, this double consciousness, this sense of always looking at one's self through the eye of others, of measuring one's soul by the tape of a world that looks on in amused contempt and pity. One ever feels his twoness—an American, a Negro; two souls, two thoughts, the unreconciled strivings; two warring ideals in one dark body whose dogged strength alone keeps it from being torn asunder." The double consciousness that DuBois describes aptly conveys the discrepancies between achieved and ascribed status conflicts that many minority social scientists experience. The crux of the problem lies in the differential rankings given to research, teaching, and services by the university, community, and individual. While the university emphasizes publishing, teaching, and service—in that order—in evaluating its faculty, the community places service first and publishing last. However, many minority professors find that teaching consumes their time and interest and believe that it should weigh most heavily.

Of course, all new faculty members experience anxiety about publication because the university gives such primacy to this area of their performance. Minority faculty members whose area of specialization involves ethnic communities are particularly vulnerable to conflicts between the criteria of the university and the community. Their consciousness of the differences between the two perspectives not only intensifies their vulnerability but frequently overshadows their need to establish in their own mind the personal standards and criteria for constructing a viable professional identity.

Expedience convinces some to adhere to the criteria articulated by the university. The issue then becomes one of the kinds of articles and the journals in which they will appear. Journals that have high status in the academic community tend to emphasize studies that further the development of methodological practices and theoretical models. From this perspective, the aspects of an ethnic community on which the researcher focuses become the means to methodological or theoretical ends. At the same time, when the researcher identifies with the group studied, the resulting work implies a self-referential level that the work of nonminority faculty members seems not to possess. Moreover, member status can also encourage the appropriation of such studies for ends other than those normally associated with publications. They are quoted out of context by policy makers and attacked both by members of the ethnic community and by other academicians for sacrificing the community's needs or interests to their own self-interest.

Minority scholars who attempt to use community criteria as the basis for publications encounter different problems. Within ethnic communities, rigorous but esoteric research is often viewed as damaging, if not worthless. The research that counts in these communities is the research that advocates change, that helps to get money, and that speaks in plain language. While such work can be judged for its inherent quality, its real value lies in the role that it plays in achieving community goals. The university tends to be unsympathetic to publications that are answerable to a particular set of cultural beliefs. It views them as too particularistic or subjective. However, this response tends to reaffirm the community's view of the university as a racist institution concerned only with perpetuating the image of ethnic communities as disorganized, deviant, or pathological. These experiences heighten the minority scholar's sense of distance from nonminority colleagues and increases his or her alienation from the university.

The vicious circle that traps minority faculty members transforms the dictum Publish or Perish into Publish and Perish. The image of the dedicated and prolific scholar that prevails in academia rules out entangling alliances with interests and concerns outside the ivory tower. The impact of pressures exerted by alternative cultural or ethnic perspectives is not recognized, and it will not be recognized until sufficient numbers of minority faculty members create a literature that can form such a view. In the meantime, the university's culture is the sole standard in evaluation for tenure.

While problems created by publications are frequently aired, the complications that arise from teaching receive relatively little attention. The issue surfaces during disputes about tenure, because minority faculty members feel that the university does not appreciate the extent of their contributions in this area. Again, the difficulty involves a discrepancy between the established traditions of academia and the modifications that ethnic diversity necessitates in that tradition.

Faculty members of color are unwittingly cast into positions of role model. When a traditional faculty member functions in that role, status is accorded in terms of discipline, not of ethnicity. In contrast, the minority role model's position is more often derived from ethnic than from academic identity. We are compelled by our disproportionately small number to accept this responsibility, and we are thrust into these positions virtually without choice. The stress in balancing visibility and role model status makes us vulnerable to pressures from both minority faculty and students. By virtue of our color, we symbolize each other, and we represent, both in the eyes of the other and in our own, each other's competencies and weaknesses. As a result, we often use criteria far harsher than traditional university standards to judge each other's behavior. In all cases, "a negative sanction [received] from one's own ehtnic group [is] far more devastating than one received from whites" (Mitchell, 1982, p. 37). The situation for the female ethnic professor is even more complicated. In addition to serving as a role model for profession and race, ethnic women must also assume the role for gender. The accountability and time demands that the female ethnic professor encounters are especially pressing, given the fact that minority women occupy even fewer positions than minority men.

The difficulty of negotiating between the university's assumptions and the students' ethnically conditioned expectations is increased by our vulnerability to student-initiated evaluations of performance. Past treatment gives students their own understanding of the institution's perspectives on minorities as members of the university. In general, such treatment has reinforced an association between minority status and low competence that activates ethnically acquired defense reactions in minority students. This reaction encourages group strategies for protecting individual members from the corrosive effects of a hostile environment. The identity shared by minority students and faculty members and the protective strategies can interfere with the critical and evaluative functions that professors must fulfill if their students are to learn. Thus, while students see university treatment of minority faculty and students as an expression of institutional racism, minority faculty members who accept this definition of the situation are hindered by students' limited understanding of the role of the professor. The efforts that minority faculty members make to fulfill that role are often misconstrued by students as attempts to deny shared ethnic identity, and students are led to interpret the professor's definition of the situation as a denial of ethnicity. In any case, whether the faculty member is seen as loyal to the ethnic group or as loyal to the university, he or she is not seen as an individual. Consequently, this dilemma becomes the primary element of our visibility and the source of great stress; the self is obscured by the social category.

Stereotypes also exist for those among us who struggle to assert our individuality and independence. Under such circumstances, we may be accused of wanting to deny racial or ethnic heritage, and we may be criticized for seeking assimilation to the "idealized" white world. The conformist directives from our reference groups and from the university lock us into symbols and images. It is not just the white academic structure that boxes us in and that sanctions our behavior according to prescribed norms and values but the ethnic community as well. Ironically, the same kind of boxing in exists within the ethnic academic community, and the demands placed on us to reflect ethnically established standards and beliefs are just as intense, if not more so; we become locked in to our ethnicity.

Students' needs, students' estrangement from home and community, and students' feelings of cultural isolation subject minority faculty to demands that encroach on scarce research time. Minority students often expect minority faculty to make themselves available beyond regularly scheduled office hours believing that they "owe" them the time because of their shared ethnic membership. Minority faculty are also expected to give more time and help, to be understanding when papers are turned in late, and to bend university standards because such standards do not reflect the minority belief system. Resentment can flair if we attempt to maintain professional standards and establish professional distance. Under such circumstances, it becomes difficult to discourage students of color from dropping by our office to chat and considerably more difficult to persuade them to seek the academic and personal counseling they need from the appropriate centers on campus. Many minority students are distrustful of and reluctant to use these resources and reject them outright. They come to us because they believe that we are better able than white professors to empathize with their circumstances academically and personally. As role models by design, we represent for them what they can become. We are the minorities who have made it. We have mastered the tricks of the trade, and we have learned how to negotiate the system successfully. They want to learn those skills from us. It is difficult for them to understand that developing such skills requires time for research, cogitation, and privacy. If we attempt to discourage them from visiting during hours set aside for preparation or research, we face resentment. Indeed, we can be scorned as "white ethnics."

Caught between pressing academic and ethnic needs, minority faculty may be forced to resort to the strategy of playing one demand against the other in order to survive. For example, in an attempt to deter students from visiting after office hours, we may plead faculty commitments; that is, we may use an institutional excuse to counter students' demands. We do, in fact, spend many hours with students. As a result, our research time is substantially curtailed. This can place us in academic jeopardy. By the same token, however, university demands consume a great deal of our time, although the administration seems to have little if any understanding of the time and emotional constraints under which we are forced to produce. The enormous amount of time that we spend with students is not taken into consideration when our level of productivity is compared with that of white colleagues. As a result, the minority scholar must plead ethnic demands to the university with regard to his or her academic productivity in the same way that he or she is forced to use institutional demands to explain and offset ethnic ones. In interacting both with students and with administrators, we deny ourselves, and we are unable to admit to personal preference, to demand social space, or to pursue individual interests and needs. In these situations, we are vulnerable to dual constraints, trapped as we are in the dilemma created by trying to treat the double bind as if it were rational.

Viability: Beyond the Reflections

The trick that minority faculty members, burdened with ethnic and professional demands that often are philosophically and culturally disparate in their orientation, must master requires disentangling and objectifying the realities of both worlds. The tension and stress experienced by minority faculty members stem largely from the absence of established images that prescribe their behavior as members of the ethnic and academic community. In this regard, we retain an either-or perspective from our history of legal segregation and social separation. Individuals who attempt to choose between the two groups remain hopelessly trapped in illusions and unavoidably perpetuate that legacy. Only those who realize that the dilemma can be resolved only by disentangling past group norms and statuses from the options available to individuals today are likely to appreciate that the way in which they as individuals perform their new professorial roles will eventually shape the norms and statuses of the group in the future. In other words, to escape the binds of visibility we need to rephrase the problems in terms that increase the bicultural awareness that enables individuals to establish the personal and professional criteria needed for building new levels of understanding in students. The process is neither simple nor easy. Bicultural awareness demands recognizing both the differences between two realities and the similarities that they share. Bicultural awareness is the view from the other side of the mirror.

I have discussed some of the ways in which ethnic communities and universities differ. For minority members to become viable, they must situate themselves in the overlap between the two environments. Ironically, the attention given to ethnic communities in the formal literature reflects the fragmented images of separate disciplinary perspectives. This makes it difficult to locate the areas of similarity between ethnic communities and academia. We also know, however, that human forms of collective organization are grounded in the need for survival. We can work to create a more coherent image of our ethnic communities in terms of the standards that they use for selecting and inculcating patterns of behavior that increase the groups' capacity to survive. Since these standards are used to evaluate members' performance, they include criteria for excellence. The personal criteria that we come to use for structuring our personal and professional life are derived from our experiences of the standards of excellence in our social environment. The fact that members of various ethnic groups have aspired to and achieved the status of academician indicates that ethnic and university criteria for excellence are compatible. Our task is to eliminate the distorting effects of our former exclusion from participation by using our knowledge of the symbolic orders of meaning within our own community to inform and expand the theoretical perspectives and methodologies of our academic discipline. The excellence that we incorporate into our teaching, research, and community service becomes the standards and values informing the future.

It is this criterion of excellence that gives individual minority professors a basis for constructing a personally satisfying balance between their ethnic and their professional identity. Such a balance lessens their vulnerability and increases their viability both in the ethnic and in the university community. As minority faculty members devise teaching techniques that enable students from diverse backgrounds to move back and forth between their ethnic community and the university, we give content to new categories of understanding. In contributing to the literature of our discipline on ethnic communities, we shape the form of this understanding. By participating in formulation of policy within the university, we demonstrate the efficacy of this new level of understanding for pragmatic action. Through our innovations in teaching and our additions to the literature, we broaden the university's capacity to respond productively to an increasingly complex world.

The differences that make us so visible in academic settings lose their social reverberations of past inequity as increasing numbers of minority faculty members confront their vulnerability and strive to link their visibility with the viability common to the university and the ethnic community. We cannot operate competently from within the set of expectations of either. Instead, we need consciously to pursue membership in both reference groups as we seek to become viable members of academia. We become viable only when we can operate effectively in our ethnic and university roles and contribute significantly to the development of both and to the advancement of self.

References

DuBois, W. E. B. *The Souls of Black Folk.* Greenwich, Conn.: Fawcett, 1961 [1903].

Ellison, R. *The Invisible Man.* New York: Vintage, 1972.

Mitchell, J. "Reflections of a Black Social Scientist: Some Struggles, Some Doubts, Some Hopes." *Harvard Educational Review,* 1982, *52* (1), 27–44.

Ogbu, J. "Minority Education and Caste." In N. R. Yetman and C. H. Steele (Eds.), *Majority and Minority: The Dynamics of Race and Ethnicity in American Life.* (3rd ed.) Boston: Allyn & Bacon, 1982.

Jacquelyn Mitchell is assistant professor in the Afro-American Studies Department and the Department of Applied Behavioral Sciences at the University of California, Davis. At present she is preparing a study on the social, cognitive, and linguistic experiences and development of three low-income black children in a public school kindergarten and in a black community daycare center.

The behavior of racism at the white institution can be gleaned from the thoughtful reports of white faculty struggling with the effects of racism.

White Faculty Struggling with the Effects of Racism

Joseph Katz

Many decades ago, the Swedish economist Gunnar Myrdal and his American associates jolted the conscience of Americans with a book titled *An American Dilemma* (Myrdal, 1944). Myrdal pointed out the discrepancy between the American creed of equality and the continuing brutal and unequal treatment of blacks in our midst. Since that time, significant changes have taken place both in the law of the country and in the behavior of its people. Yet, even the most casual observer finds persistent patterns of discrimination, including different rates of employment for blacks and whites, segregation in housing, and social separation. We might expect that things would be better in today's colleges and universities, since these institutions have often been in the vanguard of social progress. Professors and students alike are dedicated not just to the pursuit of truth but to the ideal of reflective intelligence and to the task of furthering mutual understanding. The facts of university life, however, show fairly widespread racial abuse (DeCoster and Mable, 1981), continuing underrepresentation of blacks on the faculty, social separation of black and white students, and limited help for black students in coping with the effects of discriminatory prior schooling.

J. H. Cones, III, J. F. Noonan, D. Janha (Eds.). *Teaching Minority Students.* New Directions for Teaching and Learning, no. 16. San Francisco: Jossey-Bass, December 1983.

The project on which this chapter is based confronted me with some grim facts about the persistence of neglect, prejudice, fear, and confusion among white faculty as they face black students in their classrooms. The project, which was conducted at a state institution, gave teachers an opportunity to investigate the role of racial issues in their teaching. I visited the campus on three separate occasions over a period of several days to conduct lengthy interviews with faculty and students. I repeatedly interviewed all members of project staff and participated in meetings with top administrators and university departments. The picture that emerged from my study is complex. I found no one who proudly voiced naive or vicious prejudices. Indeed, the faculty members whom I encountered were afraid and embarrassed to discover prejudicial thinking in themselves. But, many faculty tended to look away from the problems of race and thereby deprived themselves and their white students of the opportunity of becoming aware of their attitudes towards race and they deprived their black students of the essential opportunity of being treated uniquivocally as equals. My experience made one major reason why racism remains an unresolved problem quite clear: One root cause of racism is passivity based on obliviousness and numbed feeling. This chapter will disentangle that obliviousness as it affects white faculty.

Neglect and Avoidance

It is a curious fact that the lessening of overt discrimination, the abrogation of legal barriers, and enhanced access for black students to institutions of higher education have all supported neglect of the issue of racism. Many white faculty seem almost to think that the problem of racism has been solved. Occasionally, they are supported in this belief by some younger black students who, for their own spurious comfort, wish to deny the facts of the discrimination that they experience daily. The assumption that racism is waning leads many faculty to think that any special attention to their black students is itself a form of discrimination. Such professors, when asked about the distribution of grades of black students, will say that they do not want to engage in such counting. Yet, probing soon reveals that they think the grade performance of their black students is lower than that of white students. Further probing also reveals that thoughts and efforts devoted to raising the performance of underprepared students are not always pronounced. For instance, the introductory course in one science department had an unusually high failure rate; a large portion of the white students received less-than-passing grades, while the percentage of black students who received such grades was even larger. That department had rejected a proposal to improve the course by teaching it in two sections so that the failure rate due to differences in preparation could be lessened through appropriate phasing of instruction. I was told that the faculty did not want to engage in "high school kind of teaching."

As I probed further into the causes of neglect, I found that almost all faculty had been brought up under conditions in which discrimination of blacks was accepted and even endorsed by parents and other significant people in their environment. For instance, I interviewed a white professor who in high school had a black friend — a fellow football player and lover of poetry — whom he could not bring to his house. Many faculty were brought up in an environment in which there were simply no blacks; that absence suggested that there was a reason for excluding them. Almost every faculty member whom I interviewed was ashamed to find racial prejudice in herself or himself. To counter this shame, white faculty looked away from issues of race for fear of having to become more aware of their own almost unwilling prejudice. This remarkable fact helps to explain the deep impact that Myrdal's (1944) book made. It touched people's conscience of finding irrational stereotypes within themselves. The feeling that prejudice is ego-alien distinguishes American racism from the antisemitic racism found in pre-Nazi and Nazi Germany, which caused neither embarrassment nor guilt for academics and nonacademics alike in regard to the stereotype of the evil Jew. This split in the American consciousness gives us a handle that can help us to clarify feelings and attitudes.

Differences in Faculty Attitudes

There is a wide variety of attitudes among white faculty. On one end of the continuum are people like the young professor whose conscience was badly jolted when she was still in high school: Her state instituted a system of private schools in order to avoid federal requirements for racial integration. As soon as she could, she left the United States for study abroad. When she began teaching, she did so with a strong dedication to openness in the classroom. Her readiness to let black students know when they performed unsatisfactorily provided convincing evidence of her nondiscriminatory bent. (More encumbered faculty shy away from such clarity for fear that they may be thought prejudiced — perhaps as a defense against a lingering half-prejudice that they are dimly aware of in themselves.) Yet, even this professor found that her black students thought that she was not sufficiently caring. Only after she and her black and white students had shared their feelings about race did one obstacle to open communication fade. As she put it to me: "My perception of my class was that my students had been very interactive with each other. I saw the blacks as participating equally. In a group interview, black students in my class said that they perceived me to be open and receptive to discussing racial issues, but they felt that if they said everything that was on their minds it wouldn't be received well, so they didn't feel that they unfolded or revealed as much of themselves and their own value system in the course as they could have if they had felt that there was more receptivity. The issue was that, if they said what they felt, nobody really cared. The learning for me was that, even though I was being open and not shying away from issues, there was a point beyond which the black students did not feel they were willing to go. It made me aware of how much I don't know about other people — not just blacks but whites, too. I became much closer to the students as individuals. As a result of that effort, they appeared to realize that I was genuinely concerned, especially the black students, who started showing up in my office more frequently than before."

Near the other end of the continuum are professors who object to what they consider the unintelligibility of black dialect, the special clannishness of black students, and the inadequacies of black students' academic performance. In the words of one professor, "I cannot communicate well with the black subpopulation. It is apparently very important for blacks to know the right handshake, to know how to talk mumbo jumbo or whatever. There are things that I don't agree with that blacks do; for example, their vocabulary when they get together. They may be doing enough of that — talking in the black jargon — that they do not have enough practice using English. In consequence, they are poorly prepared for higher education." The professor and the students speak different languages, and because translation has barely been attempted there is a sense of threat and illegitimacy.

Roots of Discrimination

One asks why our society still seems compelled to continue mental and physical segregation based on skin color. Historians have explored the economic basis of discrimination. Images of black inferiority arose at the point at which exploitation of blacks became profitable for whites. As Fredrickson (1982, p. 16) writes, "When it became more profitable to use black slaves rather than white indentured servants on the tobacco plantations of the Chesapeake... a powerful incentive was created for degrading all blacks to an inferior status."

But, whatever the legitimacy of economic interpretations of discrimination, they should not lead us to hide from ourselves the fact that segregation provides an opportunity for expressing malign inclinations. We know that economic reasons do little to explain the Nazis' extermination of Jews. In this country, the discrimination written into the fabric of social life has kept blacks and whites so far apart that they do not have an adequate base for learning about and testing preconceptions. Very few white faculty whom I interviewed had acquaintance relations, not to speak of friendships, with blacks. There is thus a fertile breeding ground for the development of fears and for the projection of impulses and attitudes that are unacceptable and feared in oneself onto members of the "strange" group. Thus, a psychological walling in is added to economic segregation.

While one can view an excluded minority negatively, one can also project onto it qualities that one believes that one lacks or that one possesses to a diminished degree. Some white faculty whom I observed ascribed a depth of affect, emotional straightforwardness, and directness in admitting anger to blacks that they felt to be lacking in whites. While such idealization is more benign than the projection of undesirable qualities, it constitutes another form of prejudice. It places a burden of specialness on blacks and thus hinders the intercourse of people on the basis of equality of virtue and fallibility. Racial liberals need to struggle their way through to a demystification of blacks. Attitudes towards women are comparable in this regard. Under conditions of oppression, women are both denigrated and idealized. In either case, they become an object of male projections.

There is a borderline area in which unacceptable and idealized impulses merge — the area of sexual feelings. I was struck that, not much below the surface in some academics, black people and black students aroused strong sexual feelings. In the case of women students, there was definite hedging about sexual attraction. A male professor referred to his fear (desire) that black female students would find him too attractive; hence, he had to keep a certain distance. A female black student reported that she had noticed that her white professors often stepped back a pace or two when a black female student approached them. Images of black males stressed aggression (fear of aggression), but these images, too, at times merged with sexual ones.

Other emotions were closer to the surface. Some faculty expressed their fear of discussing facts of economic discrimination and disparity of income in their classes. As one professor said, "I cannot look black students in the eye when I talk about black unemployment." Faculty said that they were afraid of encountering feelings of anger among black students and feelings of guilt among white students that presentations on the economic situation of blacks might arouse. Fear of black anger, based on the professor's own guilty identification with a long history of oppression, surfaced many times in my investigation.

Thus, underlying the routinized meeting of white professors and black students in the classroom is a tangled web of feelings and emotions. A professor's disregard of the emotional, social, and intellectual situation of black students goes hand in hand with limitation of feeling, poverty of empathy, and attempts to avoid acknowledging anger and fear. Prejudice not only humiliates and dehumanizes the oppressed, it does something similar to the oppressor. However, professors who came to see their black students as full human beings were increasingly freed from the burden of alienation. Some, in the first flush of enthusiasm, seemed to want to throw content out of their classes. But, a balance was soon established. One does not need so much to talk about feelings as express them. Students want subject matter content, but they are very quick to discern and respond to caring, particularly when caring flows not from guilt but from a decently unemcumbered openness to other people. The project that I observed found it necessary first to tackle the problems of white professorial attitudes before it could proceed to its initial priority, knowledge and awareness of black students.

While white professors both overidealize and disparage black students, black professors are not immune from prejudice. However, for them it takes other forms. At the very least, self-consciousness about white stereotypes can lead black professors to be sensitive if not defensive about shortcomings that black students sometimes exhibit. I found that black professors were particularly sensitive to black students' use of the allegation of discrimination as an excuse for poor performance. To quote a black professor: "A student will say to a professor, 'You didn't allow me a fair chance in this course. Your line of thinking is contrary to that of my culture, and therefore you are a racist.' The faculty member has two alternatives. One is to confront the student and say 'You are wrong. I am not a racist!' and ignore the student. The other alternative is to bend the rules and allow students to get away with this. I say *get away* in the sense that, in many cases, they had just as much of a fair chance as other students in the classroom. My bias is that at a college level we are training students to become competitive in the job market. Therefore, white faculty have the responsibility to treat all students as fairly as they can, and they should understand the games that a black or white student plays in the classroom to undermine the teaching-learning process. Fortunately, in the situation that I described, a female black student observed the conversation and said to the black student, 'You are wrong. He has been more than fair with you, and I really don't think that he should give you another chance, because it is going to dilute the learning process and the struggle that I have had to go through to obtain this grade.' The teacher did tell me that at the time he was wavering on whether or not to be more lax, but the support of the black female student helped him reaffirm his stance."

Black professors were more outspoken than white professors about manipulativeness of the part of black students. It was part of black professors' being refreshingly free of the idealization of black students that, I have suggested, is itself a subtle form of racism. At the same time, some black professors stressed what they considered the realistic needs of black students to make it in the white world—for instance, to learn the ways of competitiveness and other behaviors rewarded in the white world. In that respect, they questioned the standards of the white world less than one might expect them to, given the fact that they can look at white shortcomings from a different perspective.

In moving toward increased equality, one can also lose some of the benefits that come from the distinctive experiences of different ethnic groups. One of my white interviewees stressed his consciousness of the difference in the behavior and attitudes of white and black students. Listening to him, I asked myself whether I was trying to blur distinctions, just as the notion of unisex has tended to blur some of the differences between men and women. Differences created by ethnic backgrounds and experiences have given American society a multiplicity of customs and variegated perspectives on common experience. At the same time, some of the differences have an artificial base. Blacks were forbidden to whites. This aroused the excitement and attraction of the forbidden. The demystification of blacks—a way station in the experience of white professors as they get to know black colleagues and black students better—will also mean the loss of seductive illusions.

I have sketched some underlying factors in black-white relations—emotions that often are more exciting, crude, and complex than what surface behavior shows. Surface behavior is subject to psychological censorship and dominated by rules of accommodation that make a kind of minimal coexistence possible. One has to have come to grips with the underlying trends for the surface to be different, too. Black students consistently report that white professors avoid eye contact with them and engage in other forms of behavior that limit contact and recognition of the contributions and thoughts of black students. The averted eye or ear is, among other things, an expression of the need to look away from and not hear the facts of discrimination. Indeed, it is probably not just a looking away from the black student but also from one's own felt guilt. The unconscious wish is that it would be nice, at least in the classroom, if everyone were white. That is the wish of the faculty member who says that he or she treats all students alike regardless of skin color. Once professors begin to change, they can become overly self-conscious about the transition. One faculty member almost inflicted eye contact on his students: "I have been very careful to maintain eye contact with students and to make doubly sure that I do this with black students. I have found that, in some instances, maybe I am overdoing it. It seems to make some of the black students a little uncomfortable, so that they will look away."

Black students often report that the professor's tone of voice or facial expressions displays disbelief or surprise when they respond correctly or otherwise show good performance. Here, the underlying prejudice that blacks are not as good as whites shows itself against the professor's conscious will. Prejudice and bending over backwards go together, and when it comes to helping, black students report that white professors offer little guidance and criticism of black students' work. The reasons for this behavior probably differ with the individual. For some, there is the fear of being perceived as too critical — meaning prejudiced. For others, a low opinion of blacks makes them feel that guidance and criticism will simply not be productive. Still others wish to minimize contact with people that their culture has stamped as pariahs. Racism is so much a part of the texture of our culture that professors will often make stereotypical comments about blacks without being aware of the hurtful impact that these comments can have on black students, particularly when they imply that blacks are less competent than whites. This is very similar to the thoughtless behavior of many professors when they address women or talk about women in class (Hall and Sandler, 1982). Part of the looking away involves white professors' ignorance of the contributions of blacks to society, including black literature. One of my professorial interviewees said that he assigned black writers in his literature classes but that he did so out of duty, not from a feeling for what the writers said. An economics professor described the persistent neglect of the facts of black economic life in the textbook literature of his field.

Possibilities for Change

My observations reveal a powerful taboo: Blackness is a forbidden territory, to which badness is ascribed. Blacks stir up fears and at the same time they exert a seductive attraction, which must be compensated by the defense of rejection. Under these conditions, how might change come about? One would expect psychotherapy to be a powerful instrument. Indeed, whether they had been aided by psychotherapy or not, some of my interviewees reported that they began to grow as persons once their attitudes towards blacks underwent change. But, psychotherapy is available only in some cases. Another way of effecting change is to increase acquaintance. The process can begin by bringing about more open discussion in class, enabling students to hear about the economic, social, and psychological facts of black lives. But, mere talk has its limitations. For some of the professors whom I interviewed, their behavior and attitudes to blacks began to change as a result of their having had the opportunity to become better acquainted with blacks. For instance, there was the professor referred to earlier in this chapter who had had a black friend in high school; their friendship was based on common interests and activities. In prolonged association, we can reveal to each other the depths of our being and transcend segregating rejection or romanticization. But, such friendships are difficult to initiate in the university setting, and in any case they extend beyond the confines of the classroom. Happily, there is another means at hand: participation in a joint project. As psychological research has shown, cooperation is achieved less by talking than by working together on a joint task when objectives are shared by all members of the group, when the group's well-being depends on joint work and problem solving. Assigning projects to teams of students in one's class, defining tasks that require a mixed group of white and black students to work together encourages people to express more of themselves in a setting of solidarity. One can also expect classroom cooperation to spill over into these people's personal lives and to lead to the beginnings of friendship.

There are reasons to believe that there are more bases for friendship between blacks and whites than we realize. Black students whom I interviewed talked at first as if there were little or no communication between black and white students and indicated that they moved in entirely different social circles. When I probed, however, it emerged that many black students had at least one or two close white friends. Thus, precedents for interaction exist, but they need strengthening. It is an astonishing fact that, in a society as open as ours, attitudes persist with such vigor that the relationships between people of different color are embarrassing, distant, and confused. Besides the intrinsic significance of deepening acquaintance and friendships, they are likely to enhance learning and stimulate interaction in the classroom.

The experience of the project that I studied shows that one effective way of countering racism in the classroom is to bring the facts of the black situation into the open in the classroom and to give black and white students full opportunity to express their views, attitudes, and feelings about them. Such expression can increase insight and change attitudes among students and professors alike.

This chapter has explored some of the resistance that attempts to resolving the problem of racism will encounter in the classroom. The resistance is formidable and deep. If it was not, the problem would not have lasted as long as it has. But, at the same time, the resistance is not insurmountable. It can be overcome by the healing power of abandoning prejudice; by the realization of people who take the first steps that they are growing as people, that they are less defensive in their imagination, thinking, and experience, and that they have a new warmth in their perception of others and — astonishingly — of themselves. The ultimate incentive is that the process enables one to become more fully human. It is an irony that the universities — those great promoters of productive social change — that have opened their doors wide to black students have in so many ways been remiss in constructing the bases for an emotional and intellectual regeneration of black-white relationships. Here, indeed, is the challenge. While there has been a great increase of commercialism and passivity in the universities over the last decade, there is also an opportunity to revivify the university's humanistic and transforming function.

References

DeCoster, D. A., and Mable, P. *Understanding Today's Students.* New Directions for Student Services, no. 16. San Francisco: Jossey-Bass, 1981.

Frederickson, G. M. "The Black Image in the White Mind: A New Perspective." *Arts and Sciences,* 1982, *5* (2), 14–19.

Hall, R. M., and Sandler, B. R. *The Classroom Climate: A Chilly One for Women?* Washington, D.C.: Association of American Colleges, 1982.

Myrdal, G. *An American Dilemma.* New York: Harper, 1944.

Joseph Katz is professor of human development and director of the Research Group for Human Development and Educational Policy at State University of New York, Stony Brook.

What variables promote success for minority students?
How can faculty exploit these variables in order to improve
these students' chances of success?

Teaching Minority Students

William E. Sedlacek

Just how important are faculty in student retention? Probably, they are very important. According to Astin (1975), students who find something or someone to identify with at a school are more likely to stay. Interviews with graduating seniors at the University of Maryland, College Park, showed that the single most important thing that students felt they had gotten out of college was not something they had learned in a course or their preparation for employment but the relationship that they had formed with a faculty member.

Student retention in higher education has received much attention in recent years (Lea and others, 1979). Retention of minority students has posed a particular problem, since retention rates for minority students tend to be lower than rates for white students (Astin, 1975; Avakian and others, 1982; Sedlacek and Pelham, 1976), and they are lowest in predominantly white institutions (Goodrich, 1978; Sedlacek and Webster, 1978). The literature seems to emphasize admissions procedures as a way of increasing minority student retention. In contrast, ways in which minority students might be helped to remain in school once they have started have received little attention. Also, the literature tends to focus on student services, such as counseling or miniority affairs programs, not on the role of academic faculty in minority student retention. Thus, this chapter will discuss the implications of the literature on minority student retention for faculty.

J. H. Cones, III, J. F. Noonan, D. Janha (Eds.). *Teaching Minority Students.* New Directions for Teaching and Learning, no. 16. San Francisco: Jossey-Bass, December 1983.

Variables Contributing to Minority Students' Success

Studies have shown that background, interests, and attitudinal and motivational variables are important to all students, but they become particularly relevant and unique when one is concerned with minority student success in school (Bailey, 1978; DiCesare and others, 1972; Gurin and others, 1969; Horowitz and others, 1972; Lockett, 1980; Lowman and Spuck, 1975; Perry, 1972; Pfeifer and Sedlacek, 1970; Sedlacek, 1977; Sedlacek and Brooks, 1972).

Based on the earlier work of Sedlacek and Brooks (1976), Tracey and Sedlacek (in press) have provided validity and reliability evidence for seven variables that are relevant to the retention of minority students but not necessarily useful in the retention of nonminority students. The seven variables are noncognitive, since they concern issues that are not traditionally considered to be related to academic or cognitive outcomes. The purpose of the line of research reflected in Tracey and Sedlacek (in press) was to identify and measure characteristics unique to minority students and their environment that had to do with their success in higher education. These seven variables—and an eighth posited by the author—will be discussed in this chapter, and information on how faculty can make use of them in teaching, advising, and interacting with minority students will be presented.

The context in which these variables are used is important. They should not be viewed as absolute attributes that are relevant to all minority students, nor should faculty assume that all minority students are having trouble. Rather, these variables should be viewed as hypotheses that faculty should use in interacting with minority students: Evaluate the feedback that you are getting from minority students to see whether it fits one or more of the dimensions. If there is a fit, then you have a potentially useful way of organizing and interpreting the information that you are getting. If there is not a fit, do not assume that the dimension is relevant to the particular student. Such a procedure allows faculty to make use of probabilities without forcing stereotypes.

Positive Self-Concept. Successful minority students have a positive self-concept. Confidence, strong "self" feeling, strength of character, determination, and independence are all parts of good self-concept. A good self-concept seems important for minorities at all educational levels where the effect of self-concept has been investigated. The minority student who feeds confident that he or she can make it through school is more likely to survive and graduate. Although minority students have had to battle incredible obstacles and setbacks just to apply to a college or professional school, they need even greater determination to continue—precisely because they come from a different cultural background than most of the students and faculty members whom they encounter in school.

In addition to the usual school pressures, the minority student typically must handle cultural biases and learn to bridge his or her past culture and the prevailing one. DiCesare and others (1972) found that blacks who stayed in college and adjusted to the obstacles were usually absolutely certain that they would obtain their degree, in contrast to those who left school. Epps (1969) found that a strong self-concept was directly related to black high school students' success. Sedlacek and Brooks (1972) found the same thing to be true of minority students in special programs at the university level. Astin (1982) also found self-concept important for minority student success.

Pfeifer and Sedlacek (1974) noted that such determination can take a form that makes successful minority students appear considerably different from white counterparts. They found that blacks who get high grades tend to have atypical personality profiles vis-à-vis whites who get high grades, according to norms based on white students. Thus, on some measures opposite use of the same predictor will select the best black and white students. The successful minority student, however, is likely not only to be atypical but also to be inclined toward and experienced in going against the grain. Conversely, blacks who resemble the typical successful white student on the same personality measures do not do well academically. Thus, there is good evidence that important cultural differences between blacks and whites affect the manner in which self-concept is operationalized.

Faculty appear to play a particularly critical role in the minority student's self-concept. Faculty tend to expect less of minority students than they do of white students (Chaikin and Derlega, 1978; Rosenthal and Jacobson, 1968; Rubovitz and Maehr, 1973; Woolfolk and Brooks, 1983). If a teacher expects a student to perform well, the student performs well, and vice versa. Too often, too little is expected of minority students, and the self-fulfilling prophecy becomes a reality. Lower expectations can take a variety of forms, many of which are very subtle. Being either particularly critical or overly laudatory of the performance of a minority student can affect that student's self-concept negatively. Neither form appears to be fair or to be understood by the student. Avoiding calling on a minority student in class or expecting the student to provide the minority point of view on a topic both present undue difficulties for the student and the student's self-concept.

Faculty members should base their treatment of minority students on the student's performance and recognize their own tendency to have lower expectations. It is important to note that minority students sometimes take longer to adjust to college than white students do, particularly in a predominantly white school (Farver and others, 1975; Kallingal, 1971; Tracey and Sedlacek, in press). Recognition that a student's racial and cultural background is relevant gives important support to minority students, since research has consistently shown that minority students, particularly blacks, tend to see their race or cultural group as an important aspect of their self-concept (Sedlacek and Brooks, 1976).

Understanding and Dealing with Racism. Successful minority students understand and deal with racism. Personal experience of racism makes them realistic. They are committed to fighting to improve the existing system, but they do not submit to existing wrongs, they do not hate society, and they are not "cop outs." They are able to handle a racist system, and they assert that the school has a role or duty to fight racism. Racism can take many forms. For example, an admissions office that has good intentions but that uses inappropriate predictors to select minority students commits an unconscious act of institutional racism. It is racism because it results in negative outcomes for minority students who are incorrectly selected, and it is institutional because it is the result of collective action. Sedlacek and Brooks (1976) provide an extensive discussion of racism and education.

Research has consistently shown that minority students who understand racism and who are prepared to deal with it perform better academically and are more likely to adjust to a predominantly white school than those who are not (Barbarin, 1981; DiCesare and others, 1972; Gurin and others, 1969). Minority students tend to know less about how the system works than white students do. Advising procedures, how to drop or add courses, preregistration, and study habits may all be less clear to minority students than they are to whites. Minority students probably have fewer family members and friends who have gone to college or to the same institution than white students do; thus, they tend not to have access to someone who can show them the ropes.

One new urban university with a large minority student population was surprised when enrollment dropped dramatically in the second semester. When staff contacted students, they found that most students did not realize that they had to register again each semester. The typical suburban white student is likely to know this. To the extent that seemingly routine procedures interfere with the academic progress of minority students more often than they do with white students, we have racism. For all these reasons, faculty should make an effort to initiate contact with minority students. Many minority students fully capable of doing the academic work could be saved if faculty helped them to deal with the so-called nonacademic matters.

Realistic Self-Appraisal. Successful minority students practice realistic self-appraisal. They recognize and accept academic or background deficiencies and work hard at self-development. They also recognize the need to broaden their individuality. Realism in self-appraisal by minorities does not connote cultural or racial deficiency or inferiority. However, institutional racism results in inferior education and academic background deficiencies among many minorities. The minority student who recognizes this and is prepared to act on it, individually or with the school's help, makes a better student (Barbarin, 1981; DiCesare and others, 1972; Gurin and others, 1969; Sedlacek and Brooks, 1976).

Minority students find it difficult to see a clear link between efforts and outcomes. How does this happen? The best explanation seems to be that the reinforcement system developed in our society for minority people is more capricious than the system developed for whites. Minority persons seem not to have as much control over their lives as whites do. Whites seem more likely to realize that if they do one thing, they will get another and so forth. For example, whites are more likely to feel that they will get good grades if they study hard and that getting good grades will enable them to move on to the next step. This progression is not nearly as clear for minority students, particularly for male minority students (Cleary, 1968; Pfeifer and Sedlacek, 1971; Thomas and Stanley, 1969). This is to be expected, because the majority culture tends to control minority cultures primarily through controlling males (Verma and Bagley, 1975).

Faculty must take an active role to ensure that minority students get honest and realistic feedback on how they are doing in and out of class. Being reluctant to approach a minority student because of personal discomfort at doing so should be overcome. Minority students are less clear than whites are about what they can expect from faculty, so faculty will have to initiate contact more often than they do with white students. Also, faculty should go beyond classroom considerations. Minority students tend to need more information on how the whole system works and on how they are doing in it than white students do. Minority students also tend to have less career information than white students do. Faculty can play an important role in clarifying and providing information about what it takes to be successful in a given field.

Preferring Long-Range Goals to Short-Term or Immediate Needs. Successful minority students prefer long-range goals to short-term or immediate needs. They understand and are willing to accept deferred gratification. Since role models are unavailable and the reinforcement system has been relatively random for them, many minorities have difficulty understanding the relationship between current work and the ultimate practice of their professions. Moreover, since minority students tend to have a harder time adjusting to white-oriented campus culture than white students do, we are not as sure about how minorities will perform at first as we are about whites. However, by the time of their sophomore year, the minorities who remain in school are about as predictable as whites. The minority student who is not ready to accept delayed reinforcement will experience a great deal of trouble in college.

Probably the biggest mistake that faculty make is to assume that minority students operate with the same goal-setting system that white students use. Minority students are likely to have had less experience in setting and achieving goals than white students have, and they tend to have shorter-term goals than the typical white student has. Therefore using reinforcement systems that assume that students know how something will benefit them in the long run does not work well with minority students.

To help minority students on this variable, faculty should both employ more feedback and use different methods. For instance, increasing the frequency of exams and using multiple-choice and essay exams along with written reports and class participation all will tend to help minority students. Returning exams promptly and making every effort to link performance and outcomes are other important things that faculty can do. Working with a minority student to set up goals that are accomplished, reinforced, and gradually lengthened is another thing that faculty can do. Minority students benefit by having exam dates, assignments, and so on clearly delineated and communicated. Reminders of expectations for the next class, the next week, and so forth, are particularly useful. The same process can also provide a structure for working with minority students to develop long-term goals.

The way in which financial aid programs are administered often works against minority students. Aid is often given as a lump sum, and it is not linked to student behaviors. One midwestern university decided to dispense its funds to minority students in smaller amounts for accomplishment of specific academic and nonacademic objectives. Students received the same overall amount, but the reward was tied to goal accomplishments, such as grades in courses or on exams, hours studied on a given day, and so forth. Students in this program then set and accomplished increasingly longer-term goals. This innovative practice worked well because it dealt directly with this variable—preferring long-range goals.

Availability of a Strong Support Person. Successful minority students tend to have a person of strong influence who provides advice in times of crisis. This individual may be a member of the student's immediate family, but he or she is often a relative or a community worker. Because many minority students do not have the support to fall back on that whites typically have and because the relationship between individual effort and positive outcome receives only random reinforcement, it can take relatively little to make a minority students drop out of or fail in school. There are generally many forces in white society to bring the white student who drops out back into the educational system, but the minority student who drops out may never be heard from again. Thus, minority students who have at least one strong support person in their background are more likely to make the many difficult adjustments required of minorities in a predominantly white school than those who do not.

Faculty can be the strong support person that a minority student needs, but several things seem to work against it. First, minority students tend to need the support person very early in their college life, even before they matriculate. Second, it takes time to develop a supporting relationship. The minority student's tendency to be unsure about how to approach faculty slows the process further and reduces the likelihood that a strong support relationship will develop in time. The recommendation that faculty should take an active role in initiating relationships with minority students should not be regarded as preferential treatment. Students should be approached and taught based on where they are. We cannot use the same model for everyone, nor can we expect to reach all students in the same way. Equality of treatment does not mean equality of outcome. If we want to reach minority students, the evidence suggests that we must sometimes employ different methods than we would in reaching white students. Faculty who make use of the variables presented in this chapter in their dealings with minority students will increase the probability that minority students will have the same chance of expressing their true ability as white students do.

Successful Leadership Experience. Successful minority students have successful leadership experience. They have shown an ability to organize and influence others within their cultural-racial context. The key here is that evidence of leadership tends to take nontraditional forms among minority students. Application forms and interviews are typically slanted in directions that yield little information about the background of the typical minority student. The typical white student who knows how to play the game will have held — and be sure to list — a wide variety of offices in traditional organizations. Many minority students will not have had the time or the inclination for such activities.

Promising students show their leadership in less typical ways, such as by working in their community or church or even by being a street-gang leader in high school. It is important to focus on the culturally relevant activities that minority students pursue. If minority students have succeeded in their own culture and are now ready to take on college, this is evidence that they can succeed.

Faculty encourage students to participate in a variety of departmental and schoolwide activities, such as clubs and organizations or working with faculty on research. These activities can be related to professional development and identification with a particular field. White faculty tend to identify with and respond more positively to students who resemble themselves. As a result of their alienation from white society and the education system, minority students are likely to express their activities and leadership outside the education system in churches and community groups. These two trends reduce the probability that minority students will show leadership in the college setting or that faculty will be aware of their leadership potential. Besides losing the experience involved in the activities and the chance to develop closer and different relationships with faculty, minorities are consequently less likely than whites to get to know faculty well enough to receive a perceptive letter of recommendation for a job or graduate school.

Demonstrated Community Service. Successful minority students have contributed to their community. This predictor is closely related to the leadership experience just discussed, since many of the successful leadership activities of minority students are performed in their own community. However, community service extends beyond evidence of leadership ability to provide evidence of an interest in and understanding of one's own background and willingness to help and serve one's people. If minority students reject their background, they will have trouble in such personal areas as self-concept, understanding racism, and realistic self-appraisal. The standard application blank and admission interview typically do not explore different cultural backgrounds and tend to miss a great deal of data in selecting minority students. A school that is interested in optimizing its selection process and the services that it provides to minority students must have knowledge about the cultural background of minority students.

Faculty can explore community service interests both to get to know their students better and to develop a link between students' academic and community interests. Many schools provide work study programs and have offices to facilitate faculty involvement with these programs. Astin (1975) suggests that having a point of identification with the institution is important for student retention. By recognizing the validity of community experience for minority students and by helping students to translate some of those needs and interests into school-related variables, faculty can make a big difference.

Nontraditional Knowledge. The eighth variable — hypothesized by the writer — is defined as unusual or culturally related ways of obtaining information and demonstrating knowledge. In a national study of dropouts, Astin (1975) found that blacks who were able to demonstrate knowledge gained in nontraditional ways through credit by examination were less likely to drop out than blacks who did not take credit by examination. The increase in student retention associated with demonstrating knowledge in this nontraditional way was more than twice as great for blacks as it was for whites. Faculty can be very important here by helping to identify nontraditional ways in which students can show their interest in a field. By pursuing students' interests, faculty can obtain a great deal of information that will be useful in advising and counseling students.

Generalizability and Applicability of Noncognitive Variables

Tracey and Sedlacek (in press) studied the reliability and validity of a questionnaire assessing the first seven variables examined in this chapter and found test-retest reliability coefficients ranging from .70 to .94 and interjudge agreement correlations ranging from .83 to 1.00 for open-ended items. Lockett (1980) reported coefficient alpha reliabilities ranging from .54 to .73 on a modified version of the questionnaire. Using principal components factor analysis, Tracey and Sedlacek (in press) showed that the variables tend to be independent of one another.

The exact relationship of the questionnaire to collegiate success differs from blacks and whites. For whites, the variables significantly add to the prediction of grades. For blacks, they are related both to grades and to retention. Tracey and Sedlacek (in press) found that use of the noncognitive variables alone yielded a significantly higher correlation with black student retention than did use of SAT scores alone. They also demonstrated the importance of predicting criteria beyond the freshman year. Studies that predict only freshman grades tend to give different results, and they tend to be unfair to minorities (Farver and others, 1975; Kallingall, 1971).

Using some of the noncognitive variables presented here, Lockett (1980) found that they correlated with grades and satisfaction with the college environment for black students. Thus, given their reliability and validity, the noncognitive variables appear to be useful in increasing

48

minority student retention. The Association of American Medical Colleges (Prieto and others, 1978; Sedlacek and Prieto, 1982) and the Mexican-American Legal Defense and Educational Fund (Brown and Marenco, 1980), among others, have use of the noncognitive variables discussed here. Brown and Marenco (1980) describe a system for scoring the noncognitive variables that is particularly applicable to law schools.

The variables may also be useful after admission. Students could be given the questionnaire before they matriculated, and students who were lacking in the dimensions related to college success could be identified. Programs aimed at particular variables could then be initiated for particular students. Thus, the institution's resources could be employed to maximize its chances of retaining minority students. The Counseling Center at the University of Maryland, College Park (UMCP) is implementing an intervention for black students based on these noncognitive variables as a part of an overall program of small-sample research-based attempts to reduce student attrition (Boyd and others, 1982). If the small-scale intervention works, it will be implemented for all students at UMCP.

References

Astin, A. W. *Preventing Students from Dropping Out.* San Francisco: Jossey-Bass, 1975.

Astin, A. W. *Minorities in American Higher Education: Recent Trends, Current Prospects, and Recommendations.* San Francisco: Jossey-Bass, 1982.

Avakian, N. A., MacKinney, A. C., and Allen, G. R. "Race and Sex Differences in Student Retention at an Urban University." *College and University,* 1982, *57,* 160–165.

Bailey, R. N. *Minority Admissions.* Lexington, Mass.: Heath, 1978.

Barbarin, O. A. (Ed.). *Institutional Racism and Community Competence.* Bethesda, Md.: National Institute of Mental Health, 1981.

Boyd, V. S., Magoon, T. M., and Leonard, M. M. "A Small n Intervention Approach to Attrition/Retention in Higher Education." *Journal of College Student Personnel,* 1982, *23,* 390–394.

Brown, S. E., and Marenco, E., Jr. *Law School Admissions Study.* San Francisco: Mexican-American Legal Defense and Educational Fund, 1980.

Chaikin, A., and Derlega, V. "Nonverbal Mediators of Expectancy Effects in Black and White Children." *Journal of Applied Social Psychology,* 1978, *8,* 117–125.

Cleary, T. A. "Test Bias: Predictions of Grades of Negro and White Students in Integrated Colleges." *Journal of Educational Measurement,* 1968, *5,* 115–124.

DiCesare, A., Sedlacek, W. E., and Brooks, G. C., Jr. "Nonintellectual Correlates of Black Student Attrition." *Journal of College Student Personnel,* 1972, *13,* 319–324.

Epps, E. G. "Correlates of Academic Achievement Among Northern and Southern Urban Negro Students." *Journal of Social Issues,* 1969, *25,* 5–13.

Farver, A. S., Sedlacek, W. E., and Brooks, G. C., Jr. "Longitudinal Predictions of University Grades for Blacks and Whites." *Measurement and Evaluation in Guidance,* 1975, *7,* 243–250.

Goodrich, A. "A Data-Driven Minority Student Retention Model for Faculty and Administrators in Predominantly White Institutions. Paper presented at the annual meeting of the American College Personnel Association, Detroit, March 1978.

Gurin, P., Gurin, G., Lao, R., and Beattie, M. "Internal-External Control in Motivational Dynamics of Negro Youth." *Journal of Social Issues,* 1969, *3,* 29–53.

Horowitz, J. L., Sedlacek, W. E., and Brooks, G. C., Jr. *Correlates of Black and White University Student Grades Beyond the Freshman Year.* Cultural Study Center Research Report No. 7-12. College Park: University of Maryland, 1972.

Kallingal, A. "The Prediction of Grades for Black and White Students at Michigan State University." *Journal of Educational Measurement,* 1971, *8,* 264–265.

Lea, D. H., Sedlacek, W. E., and Steward, S. S. "Problems in Retention Research in Higher Education." *NASPA Journal,* 1979, *17* (1), 2–8.

Lockett, G. C., "A Study of Traditional Measures and Nontraditional Measures Used to Predict the Success of Black College Students." Unpublished doctoral dissertation, University of Missouri–Columbia, 1980.

Lowman, R. P., and Spuck, D. W. "Predictors of College Success for the Disadvantaged Mexican-American." *Journal of College Student Personnel,* 1975, *16,* 40–48.

Perry, F., Jr. "Selected Variables Related to Success of Black Freshmen at the University of Missouri–Columbia." Unpublished dissertation, University of Missouri–Columbia, 1972.

Pfeifer, C. M., Jr., and Sedlacek, W. E. *Nonintellectual Correlates of Black and White Students' Grades at the University of Maryland.* Cultural Study Center Research Report No. 3-70. College Park: University of Maryland, 1970.

Pfeifer, C. M., Jr., and Sedlacek, W. E. "The Validity of Academic Predictors for Black and White Students at a Predominantly White University." *Journal of Educational Measurement,* 1971, *8,* 253–261.

Pfeifer, C. M., Jr., and Sedlacek, W. E. "Predicting Black Student Grades with Nonintellectual Measures." *Journal of Negro Education,* 1974, *43,* 67–76.

Prieto, D. O., Bashook, P. G., D'Costa, A. G., Elliott, P. R., Jarecky, R. K., Kahranrah, B., Leavell, W. F., and Sedlacek, W. E. *Simulated Minority Admissions Exercises Workbook.* Washington, D.C.: Association of American Medical Colleges, 1978.

Rosenthal, R., and Jacobson, L. "Self-Fulfilling Prophecies in the Classroom: Teachers' Expectations as Unintended Determinants of Pupils' Intellectual Competence." In M. Deutsch, I. Katz, and A. R. Jensen (Eds.), *Social Class, Race, and Psychological Development.* New York: Holt, Rinehart and Winston, 1968.

Rubovitz, P. C., and Maehr, M. L. "Pygmalion Black and White." *Journal of Personality and Social Psychology,* 1973, *25,* 210–218.

Sedlacek, W. E. "Should Higher Education Students Be Admitted Differentially by Race and Sex? The Evidence." *Journal of the National Association of College Admissions Counselors,* 1977, *22* (1), 22–24.

Sedlacek, W. E., and Brooks, G. C., Jr. *Predictors of Academic Success for University Students in Special Programs.* Cultural Study Center Research Report No. 4-72. College Park: University of Maryland, 1972.

Sedlacek, W. E., and Brooks, G. C., Jr. *Racism in American Education: A Model for Change.* Chicago: Nelson-Hall, 1976.

Sedlacek, W. E., and Pelham, J. C. "Minority Admissions to Large Universities: A National Survey." *Journal of Nonwhite Concerns in Personnel and Guidance,* 1976, *4* (2), 53–63.

Sedlacek, W. E., and Prieto, D. O. "An Evaluation of the Simulated Minority Admissions Exercise." *Journal of Medical Education,* 1982, *57,* 119–120.

Sedlacek, W. E., and Webster, D. W. "Admission and Retention of Minority Students in Large Universities." *Journal of College Student Personnel,* 1978, *19,* 242–248.

Thomas, C. L., and Stanley, J. "Effectiveness of High School Grades for Predicting College Grades of Black Students: A Review and Discussion." *Journal of Educational Measurement,* 1969, *6,* 203–215.

Tracey, T. J., and Sedlacek, W. E. "Noncognitive Variables in Predicting Academic Success by Race." *Measurement and Evaluation in Guidance,* in press.

Verma, G. K., and Bagley, C. *Race and Education Across Cultures.* London: Heinemann, 1975.

Woolfolk, A. E., and Brooks, D. M. "Nonverbal Communicators in Teaching." In E. W. Gordon (Ed.), *Review of Research in Education.* Washington, D. C.: American Educational Research Association, 1983.

William E. Sedlacek is director of testing, research, and data processing and assistant director of the counseling center at the University of Maryland, College Park.

*Teachers' effectiveness with minority students is limited by
their inability or reluctance to listen to the experiences and
feelings of such students.*

On Careful Listening

*Jean Wu
Kiyo Morimoto*

As the American student population has become more socially and
ethnically diverse, the students' educational assumptions and values
and their fit with the institution have come under increasing scrutiny.
With the exception of students in black colleges and universities,
minority students in institutions of higher education are in an environment that is predominantly white as regards faculty, administration,
peers, and even curricula. Many concerns experienced by minority
students arise from the incongruity between the expectations of university staff and the students' own expectations and hopes. Predominantly
white institutions tend to foster unity within cultures and to overlook
sociocultural effects and other influences on students' experiences and
performance. Educators expect minority students to assimilate to the
the university community, although they pay little attention to the fit of
the curriculum and to provision of support services for these students.
The sociocultural issues of campus life and the nature of social relationships for these students are seldom examined.

To be aware of the experiences of minority students calls into
focus our own capacity as teachers to empathize with and to legitimize
their experiences. The discomfort that painful and helpless experiences
arouse in us may make us ambivalent in the way that we choose to

J. H. Cones, III, J. F. Noonan, D. Janha (Eds.). *Teaching Minority Students.* New Directions
for Teaching and Learning, no. 16. San Francisco: Jossey-Bass, December 1983.

respond to students. For example, we may fear that we will confirm the futility of their struggle and our limits if we acknowledge their pain. Or, we may feel that we run the risk of intruding on their privacy. Yet, our choice to leave these experiences unexplored and unaddressed may cause these students to feel lost and abandoned. They may feel that their experiences are illegitimate, that they are at fault, wrong, immature, or inadequate because of their differences and difficulties.

Unheard Perspectives of Minority Students

Human beings live and grow in social contexts — family, neighborhood, community. It follows that the quality of the relationships that each individual experiences serves to nurture the kinds of learning that take place. Since we are creatures of context, our definition of ourself is shaped by our experiences in those contexts. Chinese-Americans born and raised in an American Chinatown may see themselves quite differently from an Asian-American person whose family is the only one in a predominantly white community. Although all these persons are recognizably Asian in appearance, their personal awareness, self-concept, and perceptions of the society around them can be worlds apart. The same is true for other identifiable ethnic groups. Being visibly distinguishable, however, adds a dimension that calls for special attention. Visibility results in experiences that all minority students on predominantly white campuses share and that set them apart from their white counterparts. To stand out for one's appearance renders one vulnerable to being singled out, categorized, and perhaps stereotyped. One is unable to change one's physical appearance, so one can feel quite helpless about the consequences of one's visibility.

Aside from this experience of being visibly identifiable, students from minority backgrounds in predominantly white institutions are likely to have different experiences depending on the nature of their own background. Minority students from nonwhite backgrounds or communities who enter predominantly white, Eurocentric institutions find themselves in extremely unfamiliar, even alien surroundings. They ask: Do I belong here? There are so few people that look like me here, will I be safe here? How am I seen? Will the world at large consider that I belong here? Who is familiar with me and my past? To whom can I turn with trust that will understand the background that I come from?

When students from a nonwhite background are also from a non-middle class background the questions may intensify. These minority students must struggle to learn to use their opportunity to obtain an education effectively while simultaneously striving to make sense of their past and their continuity with their past, which their present context may not reflect.

Minority students who come from a predominantly white community may have been the only visible minority in their home context. At a predominantly yet not exclusively white university, they meet a population of peers from their same racial or ethnic group. They may experience visibility or group identification for the first time, because there are others physically like themselves in close proximity. However, the years of familiarity created by growing up in an all-white environment may have left these students feeling that they know little about ethnicity — their own and others' — in society. They may have less knowledge about their own ethnic background than they do about other backgrounds. Yet, these students may also feel pressure both from within and without to know about their own group. They may discover or suspect that they harbor the same stereotypes and prejudices that majority society is accused of holding toward members of their own group. Avoidance, shame, guilt, and confusion can be the result. Their parents' and their own efforts to assimilate, their own ambition to achieve competence in the majority view, and their parents' investment in them can all leave them ambivalent about seeing their own ethnic group as different from majority society. When nonwhite students from a predominantly white background meet others who look like them, they may ask: Do I necessarily have to identify or feel belonging with them in order to feel authentic? I don't know them and I feel self-conscious with them; they seem to be different from me and to hold different views; yet will they and others accuse me of being prejudiced toward my own kind if I do not mix with them? Will the world at large see me as one of them because we look alike? Will I be placed in a category not of my own choosing? Who are they in relation to me? Who am I?

These questions may never have risen to the surface of consciousness before, because these issues were not salient and because self-conscious questioning was not necessary in past contexts. The following excerpt from the journal that one student kept for a course on Asian-American identity and experience expresses a sense of the struggle that one can encounter in searching for one's own voice and authenticity: "When I go home, I switch to Chinese almost immediately, but I find a lot of me I can't express. I can't say how I feel. My conversations with my family are like small talk, formal-like. Sometimes, if I stay more than a weekend, my whole way of being and thinking starts to change. I become part of the flow of things at home. I start responding to things in my parents' traditional, even bigoted ways. I get mad at myself. I start off by saying *hmmmm* to them so as not to quarrel, but I know there will always be disagreement — not a disagreement of ideas; it's more like languages stand for a whole world of their own. When I leave and come back to school, I feel ashamed of both me's — the one at home and the one that switches back and forth. I feel I betray my parents. They've made it possible for me to be here, but I have left them behind. My roommate says that everyone who leaves home goes through this, but I think it's especially bad if you have a very different culture at home, like some of the blacks and one American Indian guy that I talked to. Maybe someday it will be so painful to go through the switching back and forth that I won't be able to go home again, but, for a Chinese person, home is where you belong. If you don't have your family, you don't have anything."

Although their internal experiences differ widely, minority students may feel that their visibility requires them to become spokespersons for their ethnicity. They may feel burdened with erroneous stereotypes of what it means to belong to a particular race or ethnicity. They may feel patronized and dehumanized when they are seen and treated as members of a group, not as individuals. At the same time, they may feel unwelcomed and excluded from the academic community because they belong to a historically oppressed group. They may feel self-conscious when they do seek companionship and belonging in their own group. They may also feel pressures to conform to standards of behavior defined by a minority constituency as the only authentic position: If you are a loyal member of that minority, then you must behave "properly." They may feel isolated and misperceived in the home community that they have just left behind. In addition to wanting to fulfill their own aspirations, they may feel that they are at school to live out a particular mission of success, bringing pride and validation to their family and community, whose dreams and hopes for upward mobility and security may be invested in their education.

The presence of any one or a combination of these aspects in minority students' experience may leave them feeling pressured, lonely, isolated, and torn by conflicting loyalties, rage, helplessness, and futility. They may feel fundamentally misperceived, misunderstood, and unknown. These experiences may well compound the difficulty that minority students experience in finding their own voice in an institution that seems unwittingly to discourage the development of separate voices.

Listening and Communicating That We Hear Them

What does it mean to be heard? How is one heard? How can we learn to listen carefully and communicate that we hear? The way in which we are heard is often made evident by the way in which a listener responds to us. We can experience being heard in various aspects of what we are expressing. For example, we can be questioned and engaged in the content of what we are saying. We can experience that we amuse or entertain our listeners, or that we anger or sadden them. We can sense their boredom or disapproval. We can also feel heard for what we are experiencing in the wholeness of our being, for the kinds of sense that we are making of our world and our experiences. When we are heard in this way, we feel authentic and that we exist because we are recognized in our experiences as separate, valid, and meaning-making human beings. We feel real, our existence matters. We feel that our thoughts, ideas, feelings, and our whole essence have reality and importance. Our integrity as expressed or held in our world view is acknowledged. We all yearn to be heard and recognized in this way. If we examine experiences in life that have left us feeling alive and present, we will probably see that these experiences include the sense of being heard and recognized—a feeling that our presence has been affirmed and legitimized.

Listening is a complicated skill that is not easy to understand, much less to practice well, in teaching-learning situations. The difficulty arises because we lack understanding of what it means to be heard. We often answer people reflexively and easily—"Why do you say that?" or "That's very interesting" or "In what sense do you mean that?"—without paying much attention to the assumptions on which the responses are based. The interpersonal implications are different for each response, and they can be experienced differently by the speaker and by the listener.

The question "Why do you say that?" asks the student to elaborate and more likely than not to justify the position taken or the ideas or thoughts presented. "That's very interesting" allows one to feel that one is backing away or stepping aside to comment on the student's contribution, especially when it is difficult to discern the relevance or even the meaning of the student's comment. This response is often used as a way of buying time until one can find a way of responding appropriately or of putting the person off. In contrast, the question "In what sense do you mean that?" asks the person to elaborate on the response and to share the context from which it has come. We have a better chance of understanding and appreciating what a person says if we know something about the situation from which the person speaks.

Our listening to students emerges from our basic assumptions about people. The first assumption is that each of us is separate and unique. From the moment of conception, each of us grows and develops as a separate organism. Birth separates us from our mother, and we take on the functions of breathing and life-sustaining processes. The second assumption is that we are meaning-making organisms. Sense making is an inherent quality that is unique to us as a species. We make sense of our experiences and of our environment. The third assumption is that the sense that we make is the expression of our integrity; that is, it is the basis for our way of surviving, our way of being and interacting with the world.

Two other abilities that we possess are unique to us as a species: the ability to think about thinking and to think about our feelings, and the ability to feel about thinking and to have feelings about our feelings. These abilities make it possible for us to empathize with others. Indeed, our most important resource involves the way in which we listen and respond.

Careful listening to minority students requires us as listeners to communicate our empathy, to understand and be willing to see the world as another sees it, and to be committed to recognizing the validity and integrity of the other's world view. Empathy is important in listening. Empathy means the ability to put oneself in the position of the other person, to recognize the feelings that she or he seems to be experiencing. Yet, we also realize that what we sense about the other person is approximate, because we are separate human beings. If this were not so, we would run the risk of using our empathy to "get" or "make" others see things in our way for their own good.

Conclusion

In the final analysis, listening to students is fundamentally an interpersonal experience involving both teacher and learner in varying degrees of intimacy. Our effectiveness in listening can be profoundly affected by our ability to respond to the personal feelings related to learning. Each time that we challenge students to extend, alter, or examine their understanding, we raise feelings of risk, which can result in experiences of shame, guilt, and fear or of joy, excitement, inspiration, and involvement. When we are able to listen to, empathize with, and respond to those experiences, our effectiveness as teachers is broadened, and the learning of students is enhanced.

Jean Wu is a senior counselor at the Bureau of Study Counsel at Harvard University and a doctoral candidate in the Graduate School of Education.

Kiyo Morimoto is director of the Bureau of Study Counsel at Harvard University.

*Minority students can be helped to succeed in science through
a laboratory-centered curriculum and instructional strategies
that stress the development of scientific concepts and reasoning.*

Strategies to Improve the Performance of Minority Students in the Sciences

Lillian C. McDermott
Mark L. Rosenquist
Emily H. van Zee

Relatively few minority college students perform well enough in required science and mathematics courses to qualify for admission to professional programs in medicine, engineering, or the natural sciences. Inadequate preparation is generally acknowledged to be a major factor in the poor academic performance of these students. The counseling and tutoring programs typical of many college retention efforts have not been enough to overcome deficiencies in preparation. The Physics Education Group at the University of Washington has been engaged for the past seven years in an effort to improve the performance of minority students in the standard science courses. This effort takes a different approach: one with a strong academic focus. Although it is based in a physics department, we believe that any department in the sciences or mathematics could offer a similar program.

J. H. Cones, III, J. F. Noonan, D. Janha (Eds.). *Teaching Minority Students*. New Directions
for Teaching and Learning, no. 16. San Francisco: Jossey-Bass, December 1983.

We offer a special instructional program for minority students. It begins with a three-quarter-long preparatory course. This course, preferably taken during the student's first year on campus, is followed by a summer program and by additional courses during the second year as the student progresses through the standard physics series. The most promising students from the preparatory course are selected to serve as peer instructors for subsequent classes. Students who complete the entire program have done as well in standard physics courses as students at the university. Many have been admitted to competitive programs in engineering and the health sciences.

In connection with our instructional program, we have been investigating the difficulties that minority students encounter in the study of science and developing a curriculum that addresses those difficulties. This work, which has been carried out under a Development in Science Education grant from the National Science Foundation, has been reported by McDermott and others (1980), while an updated report should appear in the near future.

The curriculum is organized into six concept-based modules. The topics have been chosen to give students a secure background in the basic concepts, reasoning, and mathematical representations used in standard science courses. This curriculum forms the basis for our physics program for minority students at the University of Washington. The first three modules, Properties of Matter (Rosenquist and McDermott, 1982a), Kinematics (Rosenquist and McDermott, 1982b), and Heat and Temperature (Rosenquist and others, 1982), are also being used in a variety of science departments at other institutions. In this chapter, we will use excerpts from the curriculum to illustrate instructional strategies that we have found to be effective in helping to improve the performance of minority students in science.

Empirical Identification of Student Difficulties

As part of our curriculum development project, we investigated students' difficulties in science. From our research and teaching, we identified a number of difficulties that impede student progress. These are not unique to minority students, but they do tend to be more frequent and more severe for minority students. For convenience, we have classified the difficulties into three general categories: lack of understanding of scientific concepts, difficulty with scientific reasoning, and lack of facility with scientific representations.

Lack of Understanding of Scientific Concepts. Many students do not have the understanding of elementary scientific concepts that can serve as a basis for the more advanced concepts introduced in college-level science. Although the students may be familiar with the name of a concept, their ideas are often vague and undifferentiated, not clearly defined. Many students have difficulty discriminating between related but different concepts, such as heat and temperature, density and concentration, and even mass and volume. In a case in which more than one concept can apply, they fail to choose the concept that is appropriate for analyzing the given situation.

Difficulty with Scientific Reasoning. Many students have difficulty using the reasoning skills assumed in introductory science courses. One of the most serious problems is an inability to do proportional reasoning. For example, many students cannot decide whether to multiply or to divide in order to solve a simple physics problem. They also have difficulty in reasoning by analogy or in drawing logical conclusions in situations in which some variables are controlled and others vary.

Lack of Facility with Scientific Representations. Few students have developed an ability to put mathematics skills to use in a physical context. Even when students can plot graphs, compute slopes, and solve equations, they often fail to apply these skills to the solution of science problems. Furthermore, they cannot make connections between the different kinds of scientific representations (such as diagrams, graphs, and formulas), nor can they connect them with the actual objects or events that they represent.

Instructional Strategies

The curriculum that we designed helps students to overcome some of the difficulties just outlined. Certain instructional strategies that we have found to be effective have been incorporated into this curriculum. We discuss some of these strategies in this chapter and illustrate their use with examples of curriculum taken from the first module, Properties of Matter. This module contains the material covered in the first quarter of our preparatory course for minority students aspiring to science-related careers.

Conducting Instruction in the Laboratory. Many students experience difficulty in following a purely verbal discussion about a new concept. Understanding comes much more quickly if they can have some direct experiences with situations in which the concept in question plays a prominent role. Therefore, laboratory experiments are used whenever possible to introduce new concepts.

The concept of mass, for example, is introduced by experiments in which students measure the mass of common objects using an equal-arm balance. Mass is defined not in an abstract way — as the measure of an object's resistance to motion — or in a descriptive way — as the quantity of matter in a body — but operationally — as the number resulting from a measurement using an equal-arm balance and a set of standard weights. Similarly, the concept of volume is introduced by having students measure the volume of objects by filling them with standard cubes and counting the total. Precisely describing procedures for measuring a physical quantity helps students to connect concepts with their direct experience. For this reason, operational definitions are used throughout the curriculum.

When possible, concepts are introduced in such a way that they arise from a laboratory activity. The concept of density, for example, is introduced not by its definition but rather by an investigation of the ratio of mass to volume for different samples of the same substance. In experiment 8.1, which begins the study of density, the students calculate the ratio of mass to volume for three pieces of aluminum and for one piece of some other material, such as wood:

Experiment 8.1

Obtain a set of objects from the staff for this experiment. Find the mass and volume of each object. For each object, divide the mass by the volume. Compare the results.

What does each number tell you about the object to which it applies?

Many students are surprised to find that all three pieces of aluminum give the same ratio. They expect the largest piece to have the largest ratio, because its mass and volume are larger. This false expectation is linked to the difficulty that many students have in interpreting simple ratios.

The experiment, of course, displays the most significant characteristic of the concept of density — that the density of all objects made of the same substance is the same. The term *density* is not introduced until the students have had this experience and explored some of the implications of the constancy of mass/volume (M/V). When density is finally described in the text, students have already had some experience with situations in which the concept is important, and they have a ready example to call on when thinking about the new concept.

A continuing effort is made to help students make connections between scientific concepts and the physical world. After a concept has been introduced in the laboratory and discussed in the text, more laboratory work is given to expose students to a variety of situations in which the concept applies. Several examples given later in this chapter to illustrate other instructional strategies provide additional applications of the concept of density.

Scheduling instruction entirely in the laboratory is beneficial to the development of reasoning ability as well as to the mastery of concepts. Since most students seem to have been taught to value only the correct answer, not the method by which it has been obtained, it is important to insist that reasoning must always be explained in detail. To develop a student's reasoning ability, it is necessary to spend considerable time in individual conversation with the student. In this way, the instructor can find out where the student encounters difficulty and help the student to progress beyond that stage. A laboratory setting is ideal for this type of instruction. The instructor can move around the laboratory, holding short conversations with individual students on an informal basis. When a student encounters difficulty with the reasoning, the instructor can help to guide the student's thinking through a dialogue in which only enough help and encouragement is given to allow the student to proceed.

For many students, learning how to examine their own thinking takes a great deal of practice. Until students become accustomed to explaining their reasoning, the instructor may have to provide some of the essential elements in an explanation. The student must remain involved in every step in the discussion, however, and not be allowed to become a passive participant, as he or she is in a lecture situation. As students take an increasing part in classroom dialogues, they gradually become able to provide more of the reasoning themselves. The instructor's role then becomes one of listening and checking.

Developing Concepts and Reasoning Together. In teaching introductory science, it is important to appreciate that concepts are often inseparably linked to particular lines of reasoning. The concept of density, for example, cannot mean much to a student who does not realize what it means to say that mass and volume are proportional. Conversely, students who cannot interpret a ratio like density or appreciate its constancy have little chance of using the ratio properly in a proportional reasoning problem. Therefore, one of our central instructional strategies is to address concept formation and reasoning development together.

To illustrate, we give examples from the portion of curriculum that develops the concept of density and introduces proportional reasoning. In these exercises, the students' knowledge of mass, volume, and the constancy of their ratio provides a context for the introduction of proportional reasoning. Proportional reasoning, in turn, becomes part of the foundation of ideas and experience on which the concept of density is built.

The first experiment in the sequence of activities is the one quoted earlier in which three aluminum blocks are measured and their mass-to-volume ratios are calculated. This experiment is followed by the example problem that follows, which is solved in the text. The explanation given in the text leads students to think in a concrete way about the meaning of the number obtained when the mass of an object is divided by its volume.

Example problem:

Suppose we have a stone with a mass of 15 g and a volume of 5 cm^3. What is the mass of 1 cm^3 of this stone?

Example solution:

Figure 1 is a diagram of the stone. It is not a picture of the stone. It is not supposed to look like the stone. It is just something to help us think about the problem. The actual stone can be any shape.

Figure 1. "Instructional Strategies to Improve the Performance of Minority Students in the Sciences" by McDermott, Rosenquist, and van Zee

In Figure 1, the stone is cut into five equal pieces, each having a volume of 1 cm^3. If all these 1 cm^3 pieces share the mass equally, then we can find the mass of 1 cm^3 of stone by splitting up the total mass into 5 equal shares. The way to split up the total mass (15 g) into 5 equal shares using arithmetic is to divide: (15 g)/5 = 3 g. Since each 1 cm^3 has one of these shares, the mass of each cubic centimeter of stone is 3 g.

This problem illustrates one of the reasons why division is used in calculations. We know that the mass of 5 cm^3 is 15 g. We want to find the mass of 1 cm^3. To do this, we divide 15 by 5. When we want to find out how much of one quantity goes with just one unit of a second quanity, we divide. The result of division in this kind of problem tells us the amount of the quantity in the numerator for each unit of the quantity in the denominator.

The students have been led to interpret the ratio M/V as the number of grams for each cubic centimeter or the mass of one unit of volume. Later in the curriculum, there are many similar interpretations of ratios as the amount of the quantity in the numerator for every unit of the quantity in the denominator. This so-many-for-every-one-unit interpretation of proportional reasoning is emphasized whenever a new ratio — concentration, velocity, heat capacity — is introduced in the curriculum. We have found that, for ratios involving different dimensions in the numerator and denominator for example, g/cm^3, cm/sec, and so forth, the so-many-for-every-one-unit explanation is the explanation that students who initially lack facility with proportional reasoning most readily understand.

As the concepts of density and proportional reasoning are developed in the curriculum, they are applied to a variety of physical systems. For example, density and proportional reasoning both play a prominent role in the study of sinking and floating. To begin this topic, the students perform a series of experiments to investigate the variables affecting buoyancy. These experiments eventually lead students to conclude that an object will sink in a liquid if its density is greater than that of the liquid. This new knowledge of the role of density in sinking and floating is then used to provide a context for more proportional reasoning. Problems like Problem 23, which appear as homework or examination questions, are an important part of the instruction in both density and proportional reasoning.

Problem 23:

Two objectives, one red and one white, were put in a beaker of alcohol. The red object's density was 0.889 g/cm^3, and the white object's density was $.0891$ g/cm^3. Both objects sank to the bottom. The alcohol in the beaker had the following properties:

Mass	35.6 g
Volume	45.0 cm³
Density	0.791 g/cm³

A particular amount of water was added to the alcohol and mixed in. The properties of the water added were:

Mass	28.0 g
Volume	28.0 cm³
Density	1.000 g/cm³

When the water and alcohol were mixed, the white object remained on the bottom of the beaker, but the red object floated to the surface. What were the mass, volume, and density of the mixture of alcohol and water in the beaker? Explain your reasoning.

To solve this problem, students must know that mass is conserved, that volume is not, and that densities do not add. Further, students must realize that the density of the mixture must fall between the densities of the two objects. The students must thus obtain the mass by conservation, the density by the rules of buoyancy, and the volume by proportional reasoning. By the time this rather difficult problem is assigned to students, they have come a long way since their first exposure to density and proportional reasoning.

Confronting Confusion of Concepts. One of the most common types of conceptual difficulty that our students experience lies in confusing two concepts that can apply to the same situation. The failure to discriminate between related but different concepts can sometimes have few apparent symptoms and therefore go undetected and untreated. For example, a student may be able to find the volume of some object or to answer questions about the mass of a particular system but be unable to decide which concept to use in a situation in which either concept may apply. Such latent conceptual difficulty is likely to surface in a later work, where the basic concepts of mass and volume are not themselves under study but where these concepts must be used to understand new ideas or physical behavior.

Our strategy for helping students overcome difficulty in discriminating between concepts is to bring the problem out into the open. To accomplish this, we expose the students to situations in which concepts are likely to be confused. If confusion does occur, we are in a position to discuss it with students and begin to resolve the difficulty. To illustrate this kind of instruction, we will describe two situations that we use to help students to separate the concepts of mass and volume.

The students' first encounter with discriminating between mass and volume is Exercise 5.10, which comes right at the end of the introduction of the concept of volume. An experiment that immediately precedes it makes the connection between displacement of water and the volume of a submerged object. The experiment consists of dropping a series of one-centimeter cubes into a graduated cylinder of water and noting that the level of the water rises one milliliter for each cube that is added. Following the experiment, the students encounter Exercise 5.10, which asks them to separate the roles of mass and volume in water displacement.

Exercise 5.10

Does each gram of a submerged object displace one gram of water? Could we measure mass by water displacement of a submerged object? Explain your reasoning.

To these questions, many students respond with a forthright yes. These students have not discerned the different roles that mass and volume play in the displacement of water. Thus, an exercise of this type brings the confusion out into the open, where the context of the problem allows it to be discussed in a specific way.

The students then go on to perform a set of experiments in which they see that volume is not conserved when alcohol and water are mixed but that mass is conserved. They also find that mass is conserved when ice melts and when Alka Seltzer dissolves in a closed pressure-bottle. After the crucial distinction between the conservation of mass and the nonconservation of volume has been made, we ask students to solve Exercise 6.6.

Exercise 6.6

Obtain a syringe from the staff. Compress the gas inside, and observe what happens. Then, resolve the following dispute between two students:

Student 1:   I say the volume decreased. Volume is the number of standard cubes that fit inside, and fewer cubes would fit inside after the piston is compressed.

Student 2:   No, the volume is still the same. This is a closed system. Nothing can get in or out, so there is still the same number of cubes of air inside the syringe. Since the number of cubes of air inside is the same, the volume is the same.

Tell which student is correct, and then explain what is wrong with the other student's reasoning.

One of the most frequent interpretations of this compression experiment is that given by the second student. Students who reason in this way confuse conservation of mass with conservation in general, including conservation of volume (cubes of air). In this exercise, we require students to argue against a position that many of them may be tempted to take.

The students must again confront the distinction between mass and volume when they later investigate what determines whether an object sinks or floats. They need to design and perform a series of experiments to decide whether the mass, the volume, or some other property makes the crucial difference. To make this determination, they must realize that it is necessary to control the variables. For example, to explore the role of volume, they must examine the sinking or floating behavior of objects that have the same mass but different volume. After carrying out a series of experiments, students eventually arrive at the conclusion that density is the determining factor, not mass or volume alone. Following these experiments, students write a paper in which they retrace the sequence of experiments and inferences in their own words. In presenting their results, the students must repeatedly articulate the differences between mass and volume. We have found that, after this type of instruction, few students confuse the two concepts in subsequent work.

Connecting Algebra with Science. Throughout the curriculum, we stress to students that they must be able to connect mathematical representations, such as graphs or algebraic formulas, with science subject matter. In our instruction on algebra, for example, we concentrate not on manipulative skills but on connecting the algebra with the science at hand. Exercise 13.6, which follows, illustrates the emphasis that we place on interpreting algebraic expressions in terms of the subject matter context.

Difficulty in interpreting expressions is severe and occurs at a very elementary level. For example, if students are told that an object has a volume of 50 cm^3 and is made of a substance with density D, many cannot recognize the expression $50D$ as the mass of the object. Failure to regard an expression as a single quantity is a particularly tenacious difficulty, and it is therefore addressed again and again throughout the curriculum. The purpose of the instruction is to teach students that an algebraic expression stands for one number, not a collection of several numbers, and that an expression should therefore be interpreted as a single physical quantity. Exercise 13.6 is typical in that it requires students to write an algebraic expression that fits a context from science subject matter.

Exercise 13.6

A sample of air contained in a balloon had a mass of 1.2 g and a volume of 920 cm^3 in the lab. When the balloon was taken up into the mountains, its volume increased by an additional volume *v*. Write and expression for the density of the air in the balloon up in the mountains.

The answer to this question is the expression $1.2/(920 + v)$. This expression is typical of those required in many of our algebra problems in that it involves both variables and known numbers. If a problem contains only variables, in simple contexts like mass, volume, and density, it becomes very easy to write expressions by memorizing such formulas as $D = M/V$ and $V = M/D$ and by making minor modifications. We have found that, when numbers as well as variables are included, most students try to reason the problem through, not to plug values into a memorized formula.

The next major point made in our instruction on algebra is that an equation must be justified in terms of the statement that it makes about the physical world. The writing of equations that correctly describe a physical system is rarely covered in mathematics courses, but it is an indispensable skill for success in science. The approach that we suggest asks students to interpret the expression on each side of an equation and tell why the two expressions should be set equal. This example problem illustrates the approach:

Example problem:
Suppose we want to add some alcohol (density 0.80 g/cm³) to 50 g of water in a beaker to get a mixture with a total mass of 66 g. What volume of alcohol should be poured into the beaker?

Example solution:
We can solve this problem, because we know that, when alcohol is added to water, the total mass will just be the mass of the water plus the mass of the alcohol, in compliance with the law of conservation of mass. We therefore write expressions for the mass before mixing and after. If we let *v* be the volume of the alcohol added, the mass of the alcohol is $0.80v$. Thus, $50 + 0.80v$ is the total mass before mixing, and 66 is the total mass after mixing. Because mass is conserved, these two numbers will be exactly the same. Therefore, we are entitled to set them equal:

$$.50 + 0.80v = 66$$

This has the solution:

$$v = 20 \text{ cm}^3.$$

Hence, 20 cm³ of alcohol should be added.

The most significant step in this example problem is the justification for setting the two sides of the equation equal. In this case, the justification lies in the law of conservation of mass. When problems of this kind are given on examinations or homework, the emphasis is placed on the student's ability to defend the equating of two expressions to form an equation, not on the ensuing manipulation.

Connecting Graphs with Science. Throughout the curriculum, the construction and interpretation of graphs receive major emphasis. Students are given repeated practice in graphing in many different contexts. In addition to plotting data obtained from laboratory experiments and interpreting the results, students are required to connect the information given by a graph with the physical situation that it represents. Opportunities are provided to go back and forth between a physical situation and its graphic representation.

Many students have difficulty connecting the rise, run, and slope of a straight-line graph with the real world. Exercise 19.1, taken from the section that introduces graphs, illustrates how the curriculum helps students to make these connections.

Exercise 19.1

Suppose you have a lump of clay represented on the graph by point X. [See Figure 2.] A second lump, lump Y, is added to lump X, and they are joined together to form a new lump. The new lump is represented by point Z.

What does the length labeled a represent? Can the number represented by a be interpreted as the mass or volume of a particular piece of clay? If so, identify the piece of clay. If not, explain why not.

What does the length labeled b represent?

To interpret this graph correctly, students must envision three lumps of clay: the original lump X, the added lump Y, and the total lump Z. The point of this exercise is to have the students associate the rise b with the mass of the added lump Y and the run a with the volume of lump Y. They must also realize that the coordinates of point X represent the mass and volume of the original lump X and that the coordinates of point Z represent the mass and volume of the total lump Z.

Conclusion

The difficulties that many minority students experience in college-level science courses lie deeper than ignorance of facts or lack of

**Figure 2. "Instructional Strategies to Improve the
Performance of Minority Students in the Sciences"
by McDermott, Rosenquist, and van Zee**

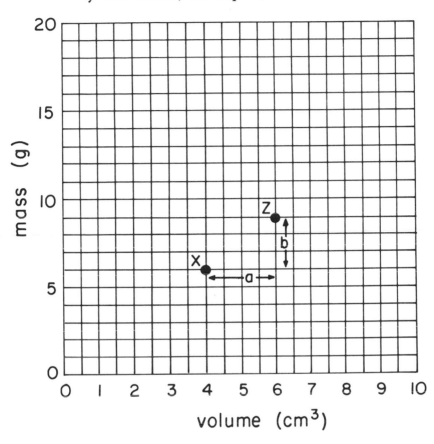

mathematical skills. For example, these students are often unable to distinguish between different but related concepts, to do proportional reasoning, and to connect numbers, graphs, and formulas with scientific concepts or physical systems. These difficulties cannot be remedied quickly by a review of mathematics or by a presentation of factual information. Rather, an extended period of instruction is necessary, one that requires both students and instructors to make an investment of time and effort.

In this chapter, we have discussed some instructional strategies that we have found to effective in our physics program for minority students at the University of Washington. To illustrate, we have used excerpts from curriculum that incorporates these instructional strategies. Our experience indicates that protracted and thorough instruction of the kind described here can improve the performance of minority students in the standard science courses required for professional programs.

As a result of seven years of experience, we believe that effective programs to prepare minority students in science should be organized around an academic core. We have found that a full-year preparatory course is necessary. In our program, this course is followed by structured tutoring while students are enrolled in the standard science courses. The most promising students serve as peer instructors in the preparatory course. Our instructional staff are always available for advice and counseling as well as for academic assistance. Thus, a strong support system is an integral part of the academic program. Although the program is based in a physics department at our school, we believe that the same approach will work equally well in other academic departments.

References

McDermott, L. C., Piternick, L. K., and Rosenquist, M. L. "Helping Minority Students Succeed in Science: I. Development of a Curriculum in Physics and Biology; II. Implementation of a Curriculum in Physics and Biology; II. Requirements for the Operation of an Academic Program in Physics and Biology." *Journal of College Science Teaching,* 1980, *9,* 135–140, 201–205, 261–225.

Rosenquist, M. L., and McDermott, L. C. *Module 1: Properties of Matter.* Physics Education Group, Department of Physics, University of Washington, 1982a.

Rosenquist, M. L., and McDermott, L. C. *Module 2: Kinematics.* Physics Education Group, Department of Physics, University of Washington, 1982b.

Rosenquist, M. L., Popp, B. D., and McDermott, L. C. *Module 3: Heat and Temperature.* Physics Education Group, Department of Physics, University of Washington, 1982.

Lillian C. McDermott is professor of physics at the University of Washington and director of the Physics Education Group in the Physics Department.

Mark L. Rosenquist, research associate, and Emily H. van Zee, teaching associate, are members of the Physics Education Group.

What happens when faculty explore their racial assumptions and try to teach minority students more effectively?

Exploring Racial Assumptions with Faculty

James H. Cones, III
Denise Janha
John F. Noonan

The favorite paradigm for improving the success of minority students at white institutions focuses attention on the students. Studies usually stress the student characteristics and behaviors that lead to academic success. However, this approach has not increased our understanding of the institution itself, particularly of how it enhances or inhibits minority students' learning. The notion of the college or university that has emerged is simplistic: Minority students move into and out of the institution. Some make it through. Many do not. But, little is known about how the college itself enhances or discourages students' learning. This notion has taken the attention away from teaching and from its impact on various students. New approaches need to be established that will help faculty to learn to be more effective with minority students.

The Center for Improving Teaching Effectiveness (CITE) at Virginia Commonwealth University has a small staff dedicated to helping faculty become more effective teachers. Its primary services to faculty are workshops and confidential consultation. Virginia Common-

J. H. Cones, III, J. F. Noonan, D. Janha (Eds.). *Teaching Minority Students.* New Directions for Teaching and Learning, no. 16. San Francisco: Jossey-Bass, December 1983.

wealth is a state-supported institution of 20,000 students, 15 percent of whom are black. About 3 percent of the teaching faculty is black.

Our work in this area started with a paper by Adelaide Simpson, a doctoral candidate in clinical psychology, who used interviews with black students to present a perspective on their learning experiences. When white faculty read transcripts of interviews or listened to recordings, they said the experience was eye-opening. Here are a few excerpts: "It wasn't just a matter of passing or failing. I knew that I had passed the course, but you always get the feeling that you have to do more just to get the pass. You never get really what you deserve, and you feel sort of like, well, my God what else do I have to do? I am always overextending myself. I always have to feel that I have to super-prove myself. Why can't they just accept me as an individual with a certain amount of intelligence and grade me on that? You are constantly faced with having to prove yourself above and beyond the call of duty, and it drains you physically and mentally—drains you to the point that, if you are not strong, you give up. A lot of students give up. They become overwhelmed."

"Several times, we would be sitting in the room with the same professor. He would go around and ask questions, and if I answered the question correctly, he would tell me in front of the group, 'Oh, you guessed, you guessed that question. You got that answer right because you guessed.' No one else guessed by me. I may have been the only one who answered correctly, but I guessed! I mean, it happened all the time. Or, he would sit in the room and talk to everybody but me. In other words, he wouldn't look in my direction."

"It gets frustrating to try to explain to people what happens, because a lot of the things that happen are emotional, but you know they are real. And, you can't explain the frustration that you feel when people say things about blacks in general that you know are not true. It becomes frustrating when you have to try to explain to white students sitting around you that they just are not true."

"I think confidence and determination have got to be the most important factors in how well you do when you get here, and if someone has their confidence destroyed or shot down by an instructor—that can be very detrimental to your learning. Sometimes, I feel that black students are made to feel that they're not capable of doing the work, and that affects their performance."

"One of the things that has always bothered me is some instructors' assuming that we are all pretty much alike. We are the same, because we're black, and we may experience some of the same feelings, such as being alienated. However, they forget individual differences.

How two, three, or four black students cope with the same environment is different, because they're different. I may cope by getting angry or militant, and someone else will accept things more readily. But, to impose one personality on two or three people is ridiculous. It's like you've got to fit into one of their stereotypes, and if you don't they don't know how to handle it. It's as if you're put into a special category."

"Sometimes I am quite reluctant to ask questions because of the put-down of the instructor. He often looks at me in disbelief when I do respond correctly. Usually, however, I don't even get recognized, and I feel, Why bother?"

"I feel like I have been through the battle and have gotten a lot of wounds, and they are well healed, but I am left with a lot of scars, and I just don't think school has to be so difficult."

In 1980, CITE received a grant from the Fund for the Improvement of Postsecondary Education (FIPSE) to expand this work through a project called "White Faculty, Black Students: Examining Assumptions and Practices." Before faculty could teach black students more effectively, we thought, they needed opportunities to explore the impact on themselves of the racism in American society. Many whites regard minorities as being the only ones who are disadvantaged by racism. We believed that whites, too, are disadvantaged, though not nearly as dramatically, when they reach middle age without having had one significant friendship with a nonwhite, when they have virtually no knowledge of nonwhite views of their field, or when all their knowledge of blacks comes from the mass media. In some important ways, we thought, white faculty have been ill prepared to teach in a multiracial setting.

The project promised faculty opportunities for self-evaluation and reflection, not a polished method to solve their problems with black students. We wanted to create no false expectations. The faculty, we believed, had to respond personally to the impressions gathered and the questions that emerged. In the beginning, some faculty saw the project as an indirect accusation that they were racist. Some were drawn to the project to get a stamp of approval. Some thought that they were helping us to conduct a study.

To start the project, we interviewed interested faculty. The interviewer's tasks were to explain the project goals, to promote candid communication, to specify how the project could be personally helpful to faculty and to explore racial assumptions. Here are the questions that we asked:

- What is your earliest remembrance of race?
- What are the messages you have gotten in your life about black people?

- How much experience did you have with blacks while growing up? As an undergraduate? As a graduate student? As a teacher?
- In what ways have these experiences affected your behavior?
- How would you describe yourself as a teacher?
- Which students do you feel most comfortable with? Least comfortable with?
- Describe a black student with whom you have felt comfortable.
- Describe a black student with whom you have felt uncomfortable.
- What stands out to you about the black students whom you have taught?
- What have you observed about the racial composition of your classes?
- What have you observed about the interaction of black and white students with each other?
- What would you like to learn from your participation in this project?

Faculty brought complex feelings to the interview, among them ambivalence, uneasiness, fear, anger, and hope. When identified, these emotions provided faculty with useful information about the impact of racism on them. Interviews lasted about ninety minutes. After the interview, many faculty were eager to continue participating, because they could pursue questions that had been on their minds for years. After the interview, we visited one or two classes because we wanted to become familiar with the teacher's style of presenting material and interacting with students, observe the racial composition and interaction in the classroom, identify teacher behaviors that appeared to encourage or discourage black student participation and black-white interaction, and develop topics for further discussion with teacher and students.

We compared what we saw in the classroom with what we had been told in the interview. We watched for subtle messages that the instructor might be sending to students, particularly to black students, through eye contact, verbal and nonverbal reinforcement, interruptions, tone of voice, posture, use of names, and invitations to participate. After the classroom visit and before the follow-up meeting, faculty were asked if we could return to the class to speak with students. We took this step to validate information gathered in interviews and class visits, to hear directly from the students' their views of the class and their experiences in it, and to break the taboo that keeps students and faculty from discussing the classroom candidly.

If the instructor seemed genuinely interested in hearing the students, we invited the instructor to join us in the meeting. Five questions were used to guide the discussion:

- What do you see as the strengths of this course and this instructor?
- What could be improved?
- How comfortable do you feel participating in this class? What makes it easy or difficult for you?
- To what extent do you see this class preparing you to function in a multiracial society? What has helped? What else could be done?
- Are there ways in which your being black or white affects your interaction with the teacher in this class? With the students?

Students were usually candid, although they were sometimes reticent at first. Some faculty learned that their fears about students' assessments were groundless. Most faculty and students reported that this part of the discussion had been quite helpful. Race begins to emerge as a pertinent issue with the question, "To what extent do you see this class preparing you to function in a multiracial society?" The question assumes that preparing students for a multiracial society is a legitimate curricular aim. It was more provocative than the first three. Racial issues differ from other classroom topics because students approach them with especially strong feelings. Statements about race can carry sensitive implications for black and white students alike. Consequently, teachers usually avoid such issues and concentrate instead on information that they can teach dispassionately. So, our raising the question often surprised the class. Occasionally, black students as well as white students denied that race was a worthwhile issue for discussion. Typically, however, black students, especially juniors and seniors, talked about race with more sophistication than whites did. Their feelings and perceptions seemed more vivid that those of the white students, who often seemed detached from the issue. White students ask, "Why can't we just talk about people instead of white people and black people?" or say, "It doesn't matter what color you are, it only matters whether you can do the job."

How did we reply? We usually invited other comments, hoping that the differences in the viewpoints expressed would be illuminating. White students especially needed help in moving to a point where they could appreciate the perspective of others. As the discussions progressed, an increasing number of students began to see how race was personally and academically relevant, and some students challenged the views of others. Toward the end of the discussion, some students asked questions about the curriculum and the practices of their department: "Why are there so few black professors?" "What are some of the other perspectives in our field?"

The style of conducting these class discussions depended on the size of the class. In large classes, it helped to divide the students into small groups. In some classes, we asked students to write their answers to the questions. Writing gave them an opportunity to be reflective and frank. Anonymity seemed to increase some students' willingness to express their views. The discussions were usually more difficult with younger, less sophisticated students. In classes where students were politically oriented, the discussion was easier to maintain. It was also easier where the course itself dealt directly with race. Classes in human relations and the humanities discussed race more readily than classes in science. Eventually, we stopped working with science faculty, because our procedures seemed inappropriate there.

After the class discussion, we met with the instructor to discuss the impressions formed in the preceding steps. By then, we had become collaborators, eager to continue learning. In the beginning, we assumed that the meeting would focus on two or three specific areas where the teacher could change to become a better teacher of black students. However, this hardly ever happened. Usually, the meeting led to more questions and to more meetings between staff and faculty.

At the suggestion of faculty, we created an arrangement whereby veteran participants could continue their own learning by teaming with a newcomer to the project. From time to time, we organized general meetings of the entire group so that teams could learn from the experiences of others. By then, the veterans had reached the point where they were ready to try something in their own teaching that would be in keeping with the project's general aims and the aims of their course—they were ready to conduct discussions of racial topics, to call on silent black students, to challenge students who denied that race makes a difference, and so forth. The general meetings tended to concentrate on teaching innovations, and the discourse was usually candid and concrete. Many faculty regarded these meetings as the most stimulating discussions of teaching in which they had ever participated.

Preparing students to function in a multiracial society requires faculty to take an active part in a project over a period of time that can be as long as several years, because they have to undo a lifetime of avoidance, ambivalence, guilt, and fear. Eliminating subtle negative signals to black students, once our main goal, is now only the beginning. The project opened our eyes to the magnitude of the problem that colleges and universities face, but it convinced us that faculty can do something about the problem if they persist in addressing it.

What advice can we give to others who want to begin their own program in this area?

- Whites should be highly visible among the leaders.
- Concentrate on educating white faculty.
- Expect resistance, but do not be stopped by it, even when it comes from a minority person who says that there is no problem.
- Insist on talking about underlying assumptions. Talking helps. Not to talk causes the problems.
- Use faculty to work with other faculty.
- Solicit the active support of key administrators.
- Preach to the converted, at least at first.
- Don't get bogged down in conducting a study. Studies can become a form of avoidance.
- Create opportunities for faculty to learn about the contributions of racial minorities to their own discipline.
- Expect that as faculty grow in racial awareness they will grow in other ways as well: by becoming more direct, more alive to different perspectives, more resourceful to all students.
- Look for opportunities to challenge your own assumptions.
- Expect to feel overwhelmed by the complexity of the problem, but persist.
- Many whites will want you to assure them they are not acting like racists. Do not provide such assurance. Part of the learning for whites lies in developing internal structures for dealing with this fear.

James H. Cones, III, is a graduate assistant at the Center for Improving Teaching Effectiveness (CITE), Virginia Commonwealth University.

Denise Janha is assistant director of CITE.

John F. Noonan, former director of CITE, is dean of arts and science at Iona College, New Rochelle, N.Y.

Hispanic college students within the university create an
academic support structure through student organization.

Laying a Foundation for Learning: Student Peer Workshop Groups

Alvin D. Rivera

There is much discussion these days about the role of high technology and how it will affect our lives. There is, however, less discussion about how members of a special segment of the population—Hispanics—are preparing for such career fields in the future. This chapter focuses on one unique approach to developing support systems for Hispanic students who are pursuing technical careers. That approach is described step by step, and the implications for educators are outlined.

Antecedent Conditions

Hispanics have been underrepresented in technical career fields, and future projections indicate that they will remain so for some time to come. While a host of reasons could be provided, one fact is clear—educational institutions (secondary as well as higher) will have a major challenge in preparing Hispanic youth for such career fields. Indeed, Hispanics are underrepresented in most professional fields. So, while this chapter focuses attention on preparation for technical careers, the concepts advanced here have broad importance for many educators—Hispanic and non-Hispanic alike—in other professional career fields as well.

J. H. Cones, III, J. F. Noonan, D. Janha (Eds.). *Teaching Minority Students.* New Directions for Teaching and Learning, no. 16. San Francisco: Jossey-Bass, December 1983.

In 1972, 2 percent of the engineers in this country were either Hispanic, American Indian, or black, yet these groups at that time constituted more than 10 percent of the nation's population. That these groups continue to be underrepresented in technical fields suggests that much work remains to be done.

Research since the 1970s has revealed some slow, positive changes. For example, the number of graduates has increased over the years. Data assembled by the National Action Council for Minorities in Engineering (NACME, 1982, p. 7) indicate that "in 1973, only 1,300 engineering graduates were black, Hispanic, or American Indian. It is estimated that approximately 3,500 minority engineering students graduated in June 1982, a 12 percent increase over 1981."

In recognition of the magnitude of the problem from a Hispanic perspective, a small group of Hispanic engineers (primarily Mexican-American) came together to discuss a possible solution. As a result of their efforts, the Society of Hispanic Professional Engineers (SHPE) was formed in 1974. The society is a nationwide professional organization dedicated to the advancement and promotion of Hispanics in technical career fields. A part of its charge is to increase the number of Hispanics who enter the engineering and science fields.

Since 1974, SHPE has focused its efforts on college students. The organization has accomplished this task by establishing student chapters on university campuses all across the country. Currently, SHPE has forty-one student chapters around the nation. Each chapter has official recognition by the educational institution at which it is located. Also, each chapter is led by officers committed to the goals of SHPE.

Because the college chapters have shown successful results, SHPE secured resources for an experimental program called Student Peer Workshop Groups. Through a modest grant from the U.S. Department of Education, the Fund for the Improvement of Postsecondary Education (FIPSE) program provided SHPE with an opportunity to experiment with its idea. In 1979, the two-year FIPSE-SHPE program was to lay a foundation for learning that profoundly influenced the activities of the student chapters involved. The FIPSE-SHPE program was later renamed. Now, it is known as the Advancing Careers in Engineering (ACE) program.

Peer Groups

Research has shown repeatedly that peer groups have a substantial influence on human behavior. Capitalizing on this fact, the energies of Hispanic students are directed in a positive way to assist other Hispanics in need of campus orientation, counseling, academic support, and other personal services.

Student Peer Workshop Groups is a college-based project. The workshop experience permits junior- and senior-year students to provide assistance to freshman- and sophomore-year students. The areas of assistance include adaptation to college life, exposure to college services (counseling, financial aid, housing, and cultural activities), academic requirements and class preparation, and career planning and development. At the beginning of the school year, all sixteen SHPE chapters involved in the ACE program submit a proposal to the program director. The proposals describe goals, activities, and budgets to implement either the Student Peer Workshop Groups activity or recruitment activity in the secondary schools. Because the students assist in developing campus projects, they tend to have a vested interest in the success of these projects.

What actually happens in the student workshops? A great variety of things that were planned take place—and many activities that were not planned. While there is great variation from campus to campus, specific activities are tailored to student needs as they are defined. In addition, each campus has a college adviser who serves as an individual resource for student activities. The activities that have been conducted include mentor relationships between upperclassmen and underclassmen, tutoring programs for small groups or individual students, and planning sessions in anticipation of academic scheduling and nonacademic activities.

As part of the ACE program, SHPE college students become involved in recruiting and orientation activities for Hispanic students. At that stage, they begin to identify incoming students. In doing so, they have the opportunity to answer students' questions and to address the needs of specific individuals. The SHPE student organization on each campus serves as a place where Hispanic students can feel that they can obtain assistance. Thus, once students' needs have been identified and their confidence has been won, involving them in the activities of their choosing becomes a mechanical function.

The second and third activities just listed are carried out in small groups. The first activity—forming mentor relationships—operates primarily on a one-to-one basis. At the University of Illinois–Chicago, students are expanding the mentorship concept. They are trying to develop mentorships in which Hispanic industrial engineers work with selected individual Hispanic college students. This activity started in spring 1983.

College administrators may worry about duplication of services. That has not been the case. In fact, the opposite is true. Students are willing to devote a great deal of energy and innovation to activities that address their direct needs. While institutional structures take time to respond to changes and needs, student organizations and groups can be a great deal more flexible. What has occurred is that Hispanic students propose activities that the university has not made available to them, or the Hispanic students integrate their projects into existing university activities. For example, on the California State University–Northridge campus, Raul C. Garcia, Jr., (1982, p. 3), coordinator of the ACE project, stated: "The mentor program was a much-needed program at our school; however, it must be interfaced with other existing programs and optimized to help the students but at the same time still provide the friendly atmosphere so important to such a program."

Perhaps the greatest contribution of the ACE program is that it involves students in their own learning experience. After hours of planning, they initiate activities based on the perceived needs in their environment. Higher education projects rarely incorporate a pioneering spirit of innovation, good use of resources, commitment to academic excellence, and firm dedication through service to fellow students. At the University of Missouri–Rolla, Russell G. Espinosa (1982, p. 18), SHPE student president, stated: "Through the ACE grant, we were also able to assist a blind student—secure three readers for classes in which the text was not available in braille. Further, the three students were picked as his readers all had a financial need." The sixteen SHPE student chapters selected for the ACE program can receive as much as $700. This money is provided by the national organization. While the sum is modest indeed, students are eager about the program, and fundraising efforts are under way on several campuses to multiply the ACE funds.

In the future, the universities will face many challenges as they strive to improve their academic standards and develop their own resource base. The ACE program, which served more than 350 Hispanic college students in the 1981–1982 school year through fourteen of its sixteen chapters, is improving the support systems in the academic climate. In so doing, ACE is helping to improve the academic standards in participating universities. Now in its third year of operation, the ACE program is unique in that, each year, the students design their own support systems.

The informal learning that takes place can be as important as the formal workshop groups. The communications, experience, and sharing support in academic and nonacademic matters alike provide students with a sense of collective identity and increase their self-esteem. More important, Hispanic students believe that the ACE program has a significant and positive influence on their lives.

In a survey that used a scale of 4.0 (strongly agree) to 1.0 (strongly disagree), the question Should the ACE program be continued in the future? was presented to fourteen SHPE student presidents. Their responses were highly affirmative, providing a mean of 3.85. Exemplifying their perspective, Sandra Aldana (1982, pp. 2–3), student president of California Polytechnic State University–Pomona, stated: "This program has greatly benefited our chapter in many ways. We have seen personal and organizational growth in our members... ACE has given the Cal Poly student chapter a goal to work for, a sense of accomplishment, a sense of camaraderie, and increased visibility on campus. The ACE program is the best thing that has happened to our student chapter in recent years."

Implications and Changes

It is not farfetched to believe that college administrators will need to be open to organizations like SHPE in the future. Moreover, given the demands that SHPE's student chapters already make, there is probably a need for more organizations like SHPE to meet the demand of Hispanies who have an interest in and the potential to prepare for a high technology career.

Higher education institutions will accommodate increasing numbers of Hispanic and minority students in the future. It is inevitable. According to 1982 data, Hispanics are one of the youngest and fastest-growing populations in the country. This finding is likely to have major implications for education institutions across the country. It will make it imperative for administrators to understand this unique clientele. In all likelihood, Hispanic students in all university academic departments will promote positive change by their very presence. They will influence needed changes in curricula and support systems necessary to see them through a successful university experience. College faculty will need to be sensitive to the new students and to learn more about them. The greatest challenge that lies before college faculty may be the need to improve their own instructional effectiveness in educating this emerging clientele.

The implications just outlined presume that Hispanics enjoy equal access to higher education. That is not the case. The most persuasive and authoritative support for this conclusion is provided by Olivas (1979). To address this concern, the ACE program supports ongoing out-

86

reach projects in the junior and senior high schools through its student chapters. The purpose of these projects is to expose Hispanic students to engineering careers, to advise them about curricula while they are still in secondary school, and to motivate them through hands-on experiences with engineering projects. All these activities help to ensure that Hispanic students will enjoy access to a career field that has long omitted them.

References

Aldana, S. Unpublished report for the Advancing Careers in Engineering (ACE) Program, Washington, D.C., 1982.

Espinosa, R. G. Unpublished report for the Advancing Careers in Engineering (ACE) Program, Washington, D.C., 1982.

Garcia, R. C. Unpublished report for the Advancing Careers in Engineering (ACE) Program, Washington, D.C., 1982.

Olivas, M. A. *The Dilemma of Access: Minorities in Two-Year Colleges.* Washington, D.C.: Howard University Press, 1979.

Alvin D. Rivera is director of the National Institute for Resources in Science and Engineering, Washington, D.C., representative of the Society of Hispanic Professional Engineers, and director of the Advancing Careers in Engineering program.

Ask yourself, How does racism frustrate my intention to teach and my students' intention to learn?

How the Mission Gets Bogged Down

James H. Cones, III

For more than two years, I have listened intently to students and faculty talking about their assumptions and behaviors where race is involved. A perspective on racism at predominately white universities has evolved from what I have heard. This perspective acknowledges the effects that racism has on teachers and students and gives clues about what teachers can do to lessen the negative consequences of racism. We can draw on the chapters in this volume as well to take a new look at how the teaching mission gets bogged down and what we can do to fulfill the teaching mission.

The way in which racism is thought to exist at predominantly white universities distracts from its robust daily reality. The typical investigation into a charge of racism looks for racist incidents between white faculty and black students. But, the assumption that directs such a search is that racism lives only in the attitudes and behaviors of individual racists. Such individuals are thought of as holdovers from an unfortunate past or as misfits produced by limited experience and distorted thinking. The way to eliminate the problem is to eliminate these people or at least to clean up their act — or so the argument goes. In some situations, the university protects problem faculty by placing

J. H. Cones, III, J. F. Noonan, D. Janha (Eds.). *Teaching Minority Students*. New Directions for Teaching and Learning, no. 16. San Francisco: Jossey-Bass, December 1983.

them in a position that makes it less likely that they will come into contact with blacks. Isolating them protects the university from embarrassment. In some respects, the identified racist can fulfill particular needs for other faculty. When the school receives complaints from minority students, it can blame the racists on campus and try to censure them. In some ways, having a certified racist makes the problem seem simple. In any case, the assumptions that racism exists in just a few individuals on campus and that it is mainly manifested by conflict between black students and white faculty sends a message that has subversive effects on education. The message says that conflict plus race equals racism. The simplistic picture that this message conveys does nothing to solve the problem.

Moreover, this picture leads faculty and students to avoid discussing racial issues. Students realize that race is a taboo topic, so they join in the conspiracy to suppress it. In effect, minority students are told that the part of their identity that is nonwhite in inappropriate, unimportant, or dangerous. Talking about who they are will be perceived as divisive. This leaves them to ponder whether their own perspective is deluded. Faculty feel that they are under the gun in their dealings with minority students. They feel that they must avoid conflict with them in order to avoid being labeled racist. At the same time, white teachers are asked to be effective with minority students. Some faculty end up withholding themselves from students because students have become a potential threat.

The success or failure of students' learning is based on what students and teacher bring to the learning moment. Neither the teacher nor the students solely determine the students' learning. Assistance can be directed at students, teacher, or both in order to increase the success of the learning. Most efforts are directed at increasing the students' readiness to learn. Writing laboratories, remedial math, and developmental programs for special students are common elements of such efforts. What they usually lack are teacher-focused strategies that broaden faculty insight and increase their teaching repertoire.

Black students and white teachers bring a complex set of expectations and a different history, values, habits, and world view to the classroom. They also bring certain abilities and deficiencies. They are intimately invested in what they bring, because what they bring represents who they are. In the teaching-learning moment, the teacher asks the student to suspend some of what he or she brings and to take on a new way of behaving or understanding. Although the student chooses what the teacher has to teach, the student asks to be acknowledged before suspending what he or she brings. When the student and the teacher are of different races, the teacher must actively facilitate the sense of acknowledgement. In doing so, the teacher conveys to the student that he or she is worthy and respected.

All students experience a sense of loss as a result of suspending past beliefs and taking on new ones. This sense of loss can be greater for the minority student who does not feel acknowledged. When this happens, the student feels angry and ambivalent about suspending the things that he or she brings to the situation. The ambivalence that the student feels can undermine motivation and keep the black student from taking on learning with total commitment at the white university. For the minority student, learning at a white school can mean losing too much.

At the same time, the teacher may be confused by the student's ambivalence. Teachers have often said to me, "I don't know what my black students want. They say they want to be treated like everyone else in class, but they don't want me to forget they are black." Teachers may feel that students do not know what they want or that they are ill prepared or not motivated. What teachers do not see is how students are threatened by teachers who know and care little about race, which is central to who they are.

Teachers can acknowledge minority students and improve their learning if they take the challenges expressed in this volume seriously. The ideas and strategies that can be gleaned from this volume will help to improve the effectiveness of white teachers with minority students. To summarize:

- Know the minority students. They enter the university with unique strengths, problems, and expectations. A teacher who knows what students bring to the institution can be an important agent of learning.
- Explore the influence of race on your teaching and learning. Find a colleague with whom you can explore the subject. Request pertinent feedback from colleagues and students.
- Conduct race-related discussions in classes where it is appropriate.
- Study minority perspectives within your own discipline. Assume responsibility for teaching white and minority students about minority issues. Make the remediation of deficiency in this area a professional priority.
- Take some responsibility for the progress of minority students. Do not rely on minority faculty to be advocates for minorities. Do it yourself. Some teachers insist that minority students need minority role models. They do. The number of minority faculty desperately needs to be increased on campuses. However, minority faculty are often too heavily relied

on to resolve the problems of minority students. If you teach minority students, you are automatically a role model, and a key question to ask is, What am I modeling for minority students?

- Be genuine and authentic without lessening your efforts to teach minorities. A teacher who makes demands on students after making them feel acknowledged will be more effective than a teacher who does not acknowledge the student but does make demands. Anger, depression, and ambivalence will frustrate the efforts of student and teacher alike when the student has to suspend what he or she brings without acknowledgement.

- Do not expect minority faculty or students to support the first efforts by whites to address these problems. Strong intrinsic incentives must be developed.

- Do not be paralyzed by the complexity of the problems. Instead of trying to find out what to think or what to say, concentrate on examining your own assumptions and practices. Do not abandon the questions themselves, as tempting as that may seem. Challenge others' assumptions as well.

- If you become enthusiastic about a new direction to pursue in this area, be prepared for resistance from faculty. People may ask why you are trying and say that they already tried it — and failed. Let their frustration be a signal for you to act. Let the frustration of minority students be a cue for you to increase your involvement and to make your caring more explicit.

James H. Cones, III, is a doctoral candidate in clinical psychology and graduate assistant at the Center for Improving Teaching Effectiveness at Virginia Commonwealth University.

The editors provide sources for further reference.

Further Reading

James H. Cones, III
Denise Janha

Astin, A. W. *Minorities in American Higher Education: Recent Trends, Current Prospects, and Recommendations.* San Francisco: Jossey-Bass, 1982.

The author examines the gains and future prospects of blacks, Chicanos, Puerto Ricans, and American Indians in higher education and makes recommendations for eliminating inequalities in higher education.

Bowser, B., and Hunt, R. G. (Eds.). *Impacts of Racism on White Americans.* Beverly Hills, Calif.: Sage, 1981.

The chapters in this book explore the causes of racism and the consequences of racism on white Americans. It fills a gap in the racism literature, which generally has focused on the impact of racism on minority groups.

Hall, R. M., and Sandler, B. R. *The Classroom Climate: A Chilly One for Women?* Washington, D.C.: Association of American Colleges, 1982.

The authors address the subtle and overt discrimination that women students face in the classroom. This book will help faculty and

J. H. Cones, III, J. F. Noonan, D. Janha (Eds.). *Teaching Minority Students.* New Directions for Teaching and Learning, no. 16. San Francisco: Jossey-Bass, December 1983.

91

administrators to understand how students' intellectual growth can be inhibited by unconscious and conscious discriminating behavior by teachers. It contains valuable suggestions for creating a healthy learning environment for all students. The problems discussed here parallel the problems in minority students in white colleges and universities.

Katz, J., and Hartnett, R. T. *Scholars in the Making: The Development of Graduate and Professional Students.* Cambridge, Mass.: Ballinger, 1976.

This book focuses on graduate students and their intellectual and personal development. Critical intellectual and nonintellectual factors for successful graduate students and the special problems of women and minority students are examined.

Katz, J. H. *White Awareness: A Handbook for Antidiscrimination.* Norman: University of Oklahoma Press, 1978.

The author analyzes the negative impacts of racism on whites in this society. She presents a structural training program to help whites understand racism — institutional and personal — and to take action to combat it. The book includes exercises that can be used both in short workshops and in more extensive training programs — excellent resource for facilitators of faculty workshops.

Knowles, L. L., and Prewitt, K. (Eds.). *Institutional Racism in America.* Englewood Cliffs, N.J.: Prentice-Hall, 1969.

This book analyzes the way in which the institutions of American society perpetuate inequities between blacks and whites despite the good intentions of many whites.

Kochman, T. *Black and White Styles in Conflict.* Chicago: University of Chicago Press, 1981.

This book explores patterns of communication between blacks and whites and the cultural differences reflected in their distinctive communication styles. "Classroom Modalities: Black and White Communicative Styles in the Classroom" has special interest for teachers.

Mingle, J. R. "Faculty and Departmental Response to Increased Black Student Enrollment." *Journal of Higher Education,* 1978, *49*(3), 201-207.

The author presents the results of a study of individual faculty and department responses to increased black student enrollment. The factors examined include curriculum changes, faculty interaction with blacks, faculty commitment to institutional support programs for black students, and the degree to which faculty altered their teaching in response.

Mitchell, J. "Reflections of a Black Social Scientist: Some Struggles, Some Doubts, Some Hopes." *Harvard Educational Review,* 1982, *52* (1), 27–44.

A black social scientist reflects on her experiences as a student, a teacher, and a researcher and raises questions about the value for blacks of the theories, research, and practices characteristic of the social sciences.

Parker, N. P. *Improving Minority Students' Competencies: Strategies in Selected Colleges.* Atlanta: Southern Regional Education Board, 1982.

A group of historically black colleges and universities report on programs to improve minority students' competencies in biology, physics, chemistry, and mathematics. The report discusses the role of faculty in developing instructional techniques, modifying courses, and establishing a philosophy of standards with sympathy.

Index